ALABASTER
GUIDED MEDITATIONS

PSALMS

READ | REFLECT | RESPOND | REST

VOLUME ONE

Guided Meditations by Kathy Khang

NLT

An imprint of InterVarsity Press
Downers Grove, Illinois

InterVarsity Press
P.O. Box 1400, Downers Grove, IL 60515-1426
ivpress.com | email@ivpress.com

InterVarsity Press® is the book-publishing division of InterVarsity Christian Fellowship/USA®, a movement of students and faculty active on campus at hundreds of universities, colleges, and schools of nursing in the United States of America, and a member movement of the International Fellowship of Evangelical Students. For information about local and regional activities, visit intervarsity.org.

All Scripture quotations are taken from the *Holy Bible*, New Living Translation, copyright ©1996, 2004, 2015. Used by permission of Tyndale House Publishers. All rights reserved.

New Living Translation, *NLT*, and the New Living Translation logo are registered trademarks of Tyndale House Publishers.

ISBN 978-0-8308-4890-4 (print)

Printed in the United States of America ∞

InterVarsity Press is committed to ecological stewardship and to the conservation of natural resources in all our operations. This book was printed using sustainably sourced paper.

Library of Congress Cataloging-in-Publication Data
A catalog record for this book is available from the Library of Congress.

P   13   12   11   10   9   8   7   6   5   4   3   2   1
Y   30   29   28   27   26   25   24   23   22   21   20

INTRODUCING ALABASTER GUIDED MEDITATIONS

In these pages you'll find an evocative pairing of photographs with the New Living Translation of the Bible. To deepen your experience of both Scripture and image, we've added guided meditations, written by experienced Bible teachers.

Lectio divina is a practice of Scripture reading, prayer, and meditation with a long and rich heritage in the Christian tradition. As early as the fourth century, the term *lectio divina* was being used by Christians like St. Ambrose, St. Hilary of Poitiers, and St. Augustine to refer to reading Scripture. The practice was developed over the years and formalized in the twelfth century— notably by St. John of the Cross, whose famous maxim says, "Seek in reading and you will find in meditation; knock in prayer and it will be opened to you in contemplation." These are the four traditional steps of lectio divina: reading, meditation, prayer, and contemplation. These steps are presented here as (1) Read, (2) Reflect, (3) Respond, and (4) Rest.

Lectio divina invites us into the Bible's world, prompting us to imagine the biblical scene, to feel what the writers of Scripture might have felt, and to listen for what the Holy Spirit might be prompting us to consider. Visio divina applies this process to images, inviting us into prayerful interaction with visual works of art. Both lectio divina and visio divina can be practiced individually or in group settings.

The Alabaster Guided Meditations combine lectio divina with visio divina, inviting us to contemplate the words of Scripture by way of the photographs that accompany the text. Readers can focus on the words of Scripture alone or add in the visual element, using the fourfold lectio divina pattern.

These meditations invite us to enter into Holy Scripture in a new way— not as a passive text to be studied, but as the living Word of God, spoken anew to us.

CREDITS

Author of Guided Meditations
Kathy Khang

Creative Director
Bryan Yè-Chung

Business Director
Brian Chung

Operations Director
Willa Jin

Product Designer
Tyler Zak

Special Thanks
Josephine Law

Photographers
Bryan Yè-Chung
Carmen Leung
Ian Teraoka
Jacob Chung
Jonathan Martin
Ophelia Ding
Roman Bozhko

Models
Alyssa Myers
Amaria Stern
Amy Jan
Eric Lige
Estevao Macario
Jae Jin
Joshua Navarro
Kelechi Emetuche
Lindsey Taylor
Megan Conner
Pamela Hernandez
Rachel Harris
Richard Wang
Samuel Sunito
Stephanie Lorraine Corrigan
Taryn Cheng

I.

1

[1] Oh, the joys of those who do not
follow the advice of the wicked,
or stand around with sinners,
or join in with mockers.
[2] But they delight in the law of the Lord,
meditating on it day and night.
[3] They are like trees planted along the riverbank,
bearing fruit each season.
Their leaves never wither,
and they prosper in all they do.
[4] But not the wicked!
They are like worthless chaff, scattered by the wind.
[5] They will be condemned at the time of judgment.
Sinners will have no place among the godly.
[6] For the Lord watches over the path of the godly,
but the path of the wicked leads to destruction.

WHAT DELIGHTS YOU?

PSALM 1:1-6

READ

1. Read Psalm 1:1-6, aloud if possible.
2. Look at the image on page 8.
3. Pause.

REFLECT

1. Read the passage again.
2. Notice the details of the image:
   - the contrast and the space in-between
   - where did your eyes go when you read the words joy, delight, day, and night
3. Read the passage again and notice contrasting words.
4. Which words catch you as you hear yourself reading?
5. Where are you in this passage? Standing or meditating? Where in your daily life are you most drawn to and why?
6. When have you joined the mockers? What did you miss by standing with sin? What shift might you be invited to make?

RESPOND

1. Think about when you last made fun of someone; then think about when you were the subject of gossip. Talk to God about why you chose to mock the other person and how it felt to be the one made fun of.
2. At any given moment we have choices to make about how we will live and how we live in relationship to others. How might God be inviting you to bear good fruit in your relationships?

REST

1. Look at the image and read the passage again.
2. If you are able, sit tall and press your feet onto the ground and your bones into the chair.
3. Inhale. Exhale.
4. Notice if you feel scattered or rooted.
5. Inhale. Exhale.
6. Know that God invites you to joy and rootedness.

2

1 Why are the nations so angry?
Why do they waste their time with futile plans?
2 The kings of the earth prepare for battle;
the rulers plot together
against the LORD
and against his anointed one.
3 "Let us break their chains," they cry,
"and free ourselves from slavery to God."
4 But the one who rules in heaven laughs.
The Lord scoffs at them.
5 Then in anger he rebukes them,
terrifying them with his fierce fury.
6 For the Lord declares,
"I have placed my chosen king on the throne
in Jerusalem, on my holy mountain."
7 The king proclaims the LORD's decree:
"The LORD said to me, 'You are my son.
Today I have become your Father.
8 Only ask, and I will give you
the nations as your inheritance,
the whole earth as your possession.
9 You will break them with an iron rod
and smash them like clay pots.'"
10 Now then, you kings, act wisely!
Be warned, you rulers of the earth!
11 Serve the LORD with reverent fear,
and rejoice with trembling.
12 Submit to God's royal son,
or he will become angry,
and you will be destroyed
in the midst of all your activities—
for his anger flares up in an instant.
But what joy for all who take refuge in him!

3

A psalm of David, regarding the time David
fled from his son Absalom.

1 O Lord, I have so many enemies;
so many are against me.
2 So many are saying,
"God will never rescue him!"
Interlude
3 But you, O Lord, are a shield around me;
you are my glory,
the one who holds my head high.
4 I cried out to the Lord,
and he answered me from his holy mountain.
Interlude
5 I lay down and slept,
yet I woke up in safety,
for the Lord was watching over me.
6 I am not afraid of ten thousand enemies
who surround me on every side.
7 Arise, O Lord!
Rescue me, my God!
Slap all my enemies in the face!
Shatter the teeth of the wicked!
8 Victory comes from you, O Lord.
May you bless your people.
Interlude

4

For the choir director: A psalm of David,
to be accompanied by stringed instruments.

1 Answer me when I call to you,
O God who declares me innocent.
Free me from my troubles.
Have mercy on me and hear my prayer.
2 How long will you people ruin my reputation?
How long will you make groundless accusations?
How long will you continue your lies?
Interlude
3 You can be sure of this:
The Lord set apart the godly for himself.
The Lord will answer when I call to him.
4 Don't sin by letting anger control you.
Think about it overnight and remain silent.
Interlude
5 Offer sacrifices in the right spirit,
and trust the Lord.
6 Many people say, "Who will show us better times?"
Let your face smile on us, Lord.
7 You have given me greater joy
than those who have abundant harvests of
grain and new wine.
8 In peace I will lie down and sleep,
for you alone, O Lord, will keep me safe.

5

For the choir director: A psalm of David, to be accompanied by the flute.

1 O Lord, hear me as I pray;
  pay attention to my groaning.
2 Listen to my cry for help,
  my King and my God,
  for I pray to no one but you.
3 Listen to my voice in the morning, Lord.
  Each morning I bring my requests to you and
  wait expectantly.
4 O God, you take no pleasure in wickedness;
  you cannot tolerate the sins of the wicked.
5 Therefore, the proud may not
  stand in your presence,
  for you hate all who do evil.
6 You will destroy those who tell lies.
  The Lord detests murderers and deceivers.
7 Because of your unfailing love,
  I can enter your house;
  I will worship at your Temple with deepest awe.
8 Lead me in the right path, O Lord,
  or my enemies will conquer me.
  Make your way plain for me to follow.
9 My enemies cannot speak a truthful word.
  Their deepest desire is to destroy others.
  Their talk is foul,
  like the stench from an open grave.
  Their tongues are filled with flattery.
10 O God, declare them guilty.
  Let them be caught in their own traps.
  Drive them away because of their many sins,
  for they have rebelled against you.

11 But let all who take refuge in you rejoice;
  let them sing joyful praises forever.
  Spread your protection over them,
  that all who love your name
  may be filled with joy.
12 For you bless the godly, O Lord;
  you surround them with your shield of love.

6

For the choir director: A psalm of David, to be accompanied by an eight-stringed instrument.

1 O Lord, don't rebuke me in your anger
  or discipline me in your rage.
2 Have compassion on me, Lord, for I am weak.
  Heal me, Lord, for my bones are in agony.
3 I am sick at heart.
  How long, O Lord, until you restore me?
4 Return, O Lord, and rescue me.
  Save me because of your unfailing love.
5 For the dead do not remember you.
  Who can praise you from the grave?
6 I am worn out from sobbing.
  All night I flood my bed with weeping,
  drenching it with my tears.
7 My vision is blurred by grief;
  my eyes are worn out because of all my enemies.
8 Go away, all you who do evil,
  for the Lord has heard my weeping.
9 The Lord has heard my plea;
  the Lord will answer my prayer.
10 May all my enemies be disgraced and terrified.
  May they suddenly turn back in shame.

7

A psalm of David, which he sang to the Lord
concerning Cush of the tribe of Benjamin.

¹ I come to you for protection, O Lord my God.
Save me from my persecutors—rescue me!

² If you don't, they will maul me like a lion,
tearing me to pieces with no one to rescue me.

³ O Lord my God, if I have done wrong
or am guilty of injustice,

⁴ if I have betrayed a friend
or plundered my enemy without cause,

⁵ then let my enemies capture me.
Let them trample me into the ground
and drag my honor in the dust.
Interlude

⁶ Arise, O Lord, in anger!
Stand up against the fury of my enemies!
Wake up, my God, and bring justice!

⁷ Gather the nations before you.
Rule over them from on high.

⁸ The Lord judges the nations.
Declare me righteous, O Lord,
for I am innocent, O Most High!

⁹ End the evil of those who are wicked,
and defend the righteous.
For you look deep within the mind and heart,
O righteous God.

¹⁰ God is my shield,
saving those whose hearts
are true and right.

¹¹ God is an honest judge.
He is angry with the wicked every day.

¹² If a person does not repent,
God will sharpen his sword;
he will bend and string his bow.

¹³ He will prepare his deadly weapons
and shoot his flaming arrows.

¹⁴ The wicked conceive evil;
they are pregnant with trouble
and give birth to lies.

¹⁵ They dig a deep pit to trap others,
then fall into it themselves.

¹⁶ The trouble they make for others
backfires on them.
The violence they plan
falls on their own heads.

¹⁷ I will thank the Lord because he is just;
I will sing praise to the name of
the Lord Most High.

8

For the choir director: A psalm of David, to be accompanied by a stringed instrument.

¹ O Lord, our Lord,
   your majestic name fills the earth!
   Your glory is higher than the heavens.
² You have taught children and infants
   to tell of your strength,
   silencing your enemies
   and all who oppose you.
³ When I look at the night sky
   and see the work of your fingers—
   the moon and the stars you set in place—
⁴ what are mere mortals
   that you should think about them,
   human beings that you should care for them?
⁵ Yet you made them only a little lower than God
   and crowned them with glory and honor.
⁶ You gave them charge of everything you made,
   putting all things under their authority—
⁷ the flocks and the herds
   and all the wild animals,
⁸ the birds in the sky, the fish in the sea,
   and everything that swims the ocean currents.
⁹ O Lord, our Lord,
   your majestic name fills the earth!

NAME GOD

PSALM 8

READ

1. Read Psalm 8.

REFLECT

1. Read the passage again.
2. Notice what actions and attributes are assigned to God. What do you learn about God in this passage?
3. Read the passage again.
4. How does the author see himself in this passage? What do you learn about the author and how does that relate to you, to us? What do we learn about ourselves?
5. What are some of the things you learned about God as a child? How has your understanding of God changed?
6. Where in nature do you see and experience God?
7. What does authority over someone or something look like? How does that responsibility look different through God's lens and care for us and then extended to us?

RESPOND

1. Write down, mentally list, or create images, sounds, or movement for the names you have for God.
2. Read each name aloud. Think about each name. Look at your list or image. Listen if you created a sound, or move if you gave the names a movement. How does each name make you feel in your body? In your mind? In your soul?

REST

1. Read the passage a final time.
2. Inhale. Exhale.
3. If you are able, take some time to look out into the night sky or lie down and imagine the beauty of the moon and the stars, taking joy and peace knowing God created you with the same care and beauty.

9

*For the choir director: A psalm of David, to be sung
to the tune "Death of the Son."*

1 I will praise you, LORD, with all my heart;
I will tell of all the marvelous things you have done.

2 I will be filled with joy because of you.
I will sing praises to your name, O Most High.

3 My enemies retreated;
they staggered and died when you appeared.

4 For you have judged in my favor;
from your throne you have judged with fairness.

5 You have rebuked the nations
and destroyed the wicked;
you have erased their names forever.

6 The enemy is finished, in endless ruins;
the cities you uprooted are now forgotten.

7 But the LORD reigns forever,
executing judgment from his throne.

8 He will judge the world with justice
and rule the nations with fairness.

9 The LORD is a shelter for the oppressed,
a refuge in times of trouble.

10 Those who know your name trust in you,
for you, O LORD, do not abandon
those who search for you.

11 Sing praises to the LORD who reigns in Jerusalem.
Tell the world about his unforgettable deeds.

12 For he who avenges murder cares for the helpless.
He does not ignore the cries of those who suffer.

13 LORD, have mercy on me.
See how my enemies torment me.
Snatch me back from the jaws of death.

14 Save me so I can praise you
publicly at Jerusalem's gates,
so I can rejoice that you have rescued me.

15 The nations have fallen
into the pit they dug for others.
Their own feet have been caught
in the trap they set.

16 The LORD is known for his justice.
The wicked are trapped by their own deeds.
Quiet Interlude

17 The wicked will go down to the grave.
This is the fate of all the nations who ignore God.

18 But the needy will not be ignored forever;
the hopes of the poor
will not always be crushed.

19 Arise, O LORD!
Do not let mere mortals defy you!
Judge the nations!

20 Make them tremble in fear, O LORD.
Let the nations know they are merely human.
Interlude

10

1 O LORD, why do you stand so far away?
Why do you hide when I am in trouble?

2 The wicked arrogantly hunt down the poor.
Let them be caught in the evil they plan for others.

3 For they brag about their evil desires;
they praise the greedy and curse the LORD.

4 The wicked are too proud to seek God.
They seem to think that God is dead.

5 Yet they succeed in everything they do.
They do not see your punishment awaiting them.
They sneer at all their enemies.
6 They think, "Nothing bad will ever happen to us!
We will be free of trouble forever!"
7 Their mouths are full of cursing, lies, and threats.
Trouble and evil are on the tips of their tongues.
8 They lurk in ambush in the villages,
waiting to murder innocent people.
They are always searching for helpless victims.
9 Like lions crouched in hiding,
they wait to pounce on the helpless.
Like hunters they capture the helpless
and drag them away in nets.
10 Their helpless victims are crushed;
they fall beneath the strength of the wicked.
11 The wicked think, "God isn't watching us!
He has closed his eyes and
won't even see what we do!"
12 Arise, O Lord!
Punish the wicked, O God!
Do not ignore the helpless!
13 Why do the wicked get away with despising God?
They think, "God will never call us to account."
14 But you see the trouble and grief they cause.
You take note of it and punish them.
The helpless put their trust in you.
You defend the orphans.
15 Break the arms of these wicked, evil people!
Go after them until the last one is destroyed.
16 The Lord is king forever and ever!
The godless nations will vanish from the land.
17 Lord, you know the hopes of the helpless.
Surely you will hear their cries and comfort them.
18 You will bring justice to the
orphans and the oppressed,
so mere people can no longer terrify them.

11

For the choir director: A psalm of David.

1 I trust in the Lord for protection.
So why do you say to me,
"Fly like a bird to the mountains for safety!
2 The wicked are stringing their bows
and fitting their arrows on the bowstrings.
They shoot from the shadows
at those whose hearts are right.
3 The foundations of law
and order have collapsed.
What can the righteous do?"
4 But the Lord is in his holy Temple;
the Lord still rules from heaven.
He watches everyone closely,
examining every person on earth.
5 The Lord examines both
the righteous and the wicked.
He hates those who love violence.
6 He will rain down blazing coals
and burning sulfur on the wicked,
punishing them with scorching winds.
7 For the righteous Lord loves justice.
The virtuous will see his face.

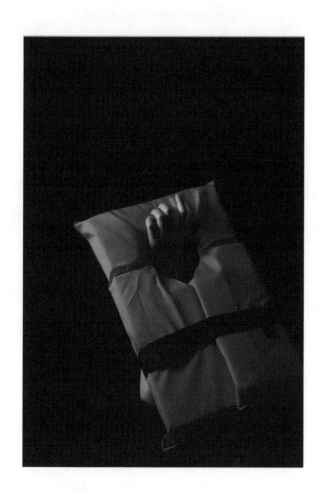

12

For the choir director: A psalm of David, to be accompanied by an eight-stringed instrument.

1 Help, O Lord, for the godly are fast disappearing!
The faithful have vanished from the earth!
2 Neighbors lie to each other,
speaking with flattering lips and deceitful hearts.
3 May the Lord cut off their flattering lips
and silence their boastful tongues.
4 They say, "We will lie to our hearts' content.
Our lips are our own—who can stop us?"
5 The Lord replies, "I have seen violence
done to the helpless,
and I have heard the groans of the poor.
Now I will rise up to rescue them,
as they have longed for me to do."
6 The Lord's promises are pure,
like silver refined in a furnace,
purified seven times over.
7 Therefore, Lord, we know
you will protect the oppressed,
preserving them forever from this lying generation,
8 even though the wicked strut about,
and evil is praised throughout the land.

13

For the choir director: A psalm of David.

1 O Lord, how long will you forget me? Forever?
How long will you look the other way?
2 How long must I struggle
with anguish in my soul,
with sorrow in my heart every day?
How long will my enemy have the upper hand?
3 Turn and answer me, O Lord my God!
Restore the sparkle to my eyes, or I will die.
4 Don't let my enemies gloat, saying,
"We have defeated him!"
Don't let them rejoice at my downfall.
5 But I trust in your unfailing love.
I will rejoice because you have rescued me.
6 I will sing to the Lord because he is good to me.

14

For the choir director: A psalm of David.

1 Only fools say in their hearts,
"There is no God."
They are corrupt, and their actions are evil;
not one of them does good!
2 The Lord looks down from heaven
on the entire human race;
he looks to see if anyone is truly wise,
if anyone seeks God.
3 But no, all have turned away;
all have become corrupt.
No one does good, not a single one!
4 Will those who do evil never learn?
They eat up my people like bread
and wouldn't think of praying to the Lord.
5 Terror will grip them,
for God is with those who obey him.
6 The wicked frustrate the plans of the oppressed,
but the Lord will protect his people.
7 Who will come from Mount Zion to rescue Israel?
When the Lord restores his people,
Jacob will shout with joy, and Israel will rejoice.

EYES TO SEE

PSALM 12:5-8

READ

1. Read Psalm 12:5-8, intentionally pausing between each verse.

REFLECT

1. Read the passage again, noticing which words or phrases catch your attention.
2. Who are the helpless and poor in this passage? Where and who are the helpless and poor in your community?
3. How are you and how are you not helpless? Poor? Oppressed?
4. How is our present generation like that mentioned in verse 7?
5. What is God's response to oppression?

RESPOND

1. Read the passage again.
2. Inhale. Exhale.
3. Notice if the same words or phrases catch your attention or invite you to ask more questions.

4. Take some time to acknowledge and confess the violence in you, in your family and home, in your community, in your church, in your country, in the world. Confess the ways you have participated in the violence done to the helpless. Consider how God is moving you into new beliefs and behaviors.
5. Name the places in your life when you have survived violence and oppression, receiving or acknowledging the rescue and protection God offers.
6. Inhale. Exhale.

REST

1. Read the passage for a final time.
2. Thank God for his promises; list them if you are so led. Thank God, who is our protector even as we identify the evil in our own generation.

15

A psalm of David.

1 Who may worship in your sanctuary, Lord?
  Who may enter your presence on your holy hill?

2 Those who lead blameless lives and do what is right,
  speaking the truth from sincere hearts.

3 Those who refuse to gossip
  or harm their neighbors
  or speak evil of their friends.

4 Those who despise flagrant sinners,
  and honor the faithful followers of the Lord,
  and keep their promises even when it hurts.

5 Those who lend money without charging interest,
  and who cannot be bribed
  to lie about the innocent.
  Such people will stand firm forever.

16

A psalm of David.

1 Keep me safe, O God,
for I have come to you for refuge.
2 I said to the LORD, "You are my Master!
Every good thing I have comes from you."
3 The godly people in the land are my true heroes!
I take pleasure in them!
4 Troubles multiply for those
who chase after other gods.
I will not take part in their sacrifices of blood
or even speak the names of their gods.
5 LORD, you alone are my inheritance,
my cup of blessing.
You guard all that is mine.
6 The land you have given me is a pleasant land.
What a wonderful inheritance!
7 I will bless the LORD who guides me;
even at night my heart instructs me.
8 I know the LORD is always with me.
I will not be shaken, for he is right beside me.
9 No wonder my heart is glad, and I rejoice.
My body rests in safety.
10 For you will not leave my soul among the dead
or allow your holy one to rot in the grave.
11 You will show me the way of life,
granting me the joy of your presence
and the pleasures of living with you forever.

17

A prayer of David.

1 O LORD, hear my plea for justice.
Listen to my cry for help.
Pay attention to my prayer,
for it comes from honest lips.
2 Declare me innocent,
for you see those who do right.
3 You have tested my thoughts
and examined my heart in the night.
You have scrutinized me and found nothing wrong.
I am determined not to sin in what I say.
4 I have followed your commands,
which keep me from following cruel and evil people.
5 My steps have stayed on your path;
I have not wavered from following you.
6 I am praying to you because I know
you will answer, O God.
Bend down and listen as I pray.
7 Show me your unfailing love in wonderful ways.
By your mighty power you rescue
those who seek refuge from their enemies.
8 Guard me as you would guard your own eyes.
Hide me in the shadow of your wings.
9 Protect me from wicked people who attack me,
from murderous enemies who surround me.
10 They are without pity. Listen to their boasting!
11 They track me down and surround me,
watching for the chance to throw me to the ground.
12 They are like hungry lions,
eager to tear me apart—
like young lions hiding in ambush.
13 Arise, O LORD!
Stand against them, and bring them to their knees!
Rescue me from the wicked with your sword!
14 By the power of your hand, O LORD,
destroy those who look to
this world for their reward.
But satisfy the hunger of your treasured ones.
May their children have plenty,
leaving an inheritance for their descendants.
15 Because I am righteous, I will see you.
When I awake, I will see you
face to face and be satisfied.

18

For the choir director: A psalm of David, the servant of the Lord. He sang this song to the Lord on the day the Lord rescued him from all his enemies and from Saul. He sang:

1 I love you, Lord;
   you are my strength.
2 The Lord is my rock,
   my fortress, and my savior;
   my God is my rock, in whom I find protection.
   He is my shield, the power that saves me,
   and my place of safety.
3 I called on the Lord, who is worthy of praise,
   and he saved me from my enemies.
4 The ropes of death entangled me;
   floods of destruction swept over me.
5 The grave wrapped its ropes around me;
   death laid a trap in my path.
6 But in my distress I cried out to the Lord;
   yes, I prayed to my God for help.
   He heard me from his sanctuary;
   my cry to him reached his ears.
7 Then the earth quaked and trembled.
   The foundations of the mountains shook;
   they quaked because of his anger.
8 Smoke poured from his nostrils;
   fierce flames leaped from his mouth.
   Glowing coals blazed forth from him.
9 He opened the heavens and came down;
   dark storm clouds were beneath his feet.
10 Mounted on a mighty angelic being, he flew,
   soaring on the wings of the wind.
11 He shrouded himself in darkness,
   veiling his approach with dark rain clouds.
12 Thick clouds shielded the brightness around him
   and rained down hail and burning coals.
13 The Lord thundered from heaven;
   the voice of the Most High resounded
   amid the hail and burning coals.
14 He shot his arrows and scattered his enemies;
   great bolts of lightning flashed,
   and they were confused.
15 Then at your command, O Lord,
   at the blast of your breath,
   the bottom of the sea could be seen,
   and the foundations of the earth were laid bare.
16 He reached down from heaven and rescued me;
   he drew me out of deep waters.
17 He rescued me from my powerful enemies,
   from those who hated me
   and were too strong for me.
18 They attacked me at a moment
   when I was in distress,
   but the Lord supported me.
19 He led me to a place of safety;
   he rescued me because he delights in me.
20 The Lord rewarded me for doing right;
   he restored me because of my innocence.
21 For I have kept the ways of the Lord;
   I have not turned from my God to follow evil.
22 I have followed all his regulations;
   I have never abandoned his decrees.
23 I am blameless before God;
   I have kept myself from sin.
24 The Lord rewarded me for doing right.

He has seen my innocence.

25 To the faithful you show yourself faithful;
to those with integrity you show integrity.

26 To the pure you show yourself pure,
but to the crooked you show yourself shrewd.

27 You rescue the humble,
but you humiliate the proud.

28 You light a lamp for me.
The LORD, my God, lights up my darkness.

29 In your strength I can crush an army;
with my God I can scale any wall.

30 God's way is perfect.
All the LORD's promises prove true.
He is a shield for all who
look to him for protection.

31 For who is God except the LORD?
Who but our God is a solid rock?

32 God arms me with strength,
and he makes my way perfect.

33 He makes me as surefooted as a deer,
enabling me to stand on mountain heights.

34 He trains my hands for battle;
he strengthens my arm to draw a bronze bow.

35 You have given me your shield of victory.
Your right hand supports me;
your help has made me great.

36 You have made a wide path for my feet
to keep them from slipping.

37 I chased my enemies and caught them;
I did not stop until they were conquered.

38 I struck them down so they could not get up;
they fell beneath my feet.

39 You have armed me with strength for the battle;
you have subdued my enemies under my feet.

40 You placed my foot on their necks.
I have destroyed all who hated me.

41 They called for help,
but no one came to their rescue.
They even cried to the LORD,
but he refused to answer.

42 I ground them as fine as dust in the wind.
I swept them into the gutter like dirt.

43 You gave me victory over my accusers.
You appointed me ruler over nations;
people I don't even know now serve me.

44 As soon as they hear of me, they submit;
foreign nations cringe before me.

45 They all lose their courage
and come trembling from their strongholds.

46 The LORD lives! Praise to my Rock!
May the God of my salvation be exalted!

47 He is the God who
pays back those who harm me;
he subdues the nations under me

48 and rescues me from my enemies.
You hold me safe beyond
the reach of my enemies;
you save me from violent opponents.

49 For this, O LORD,
I will praise you among the nations;
I will sing praises to your name.

50 You give great victories to your king;
you show unfailing love to your anointed,
to David and all his descendants forever.

19

For the choir director: A psalm of David.

¹ The heavens proclaim the glory of God.
The skies display his craftsmanship.

² Day after day they continue to speak;
night after night they make him known.

³ They speak without a sound or word;
their voice is never heard.

⁴ Yet their message has gone throughout the earth,
and their words to all the world.
God has made a home in the heavens for the sun.

⁵ It bursts forth like a radiant
bridegroom after his wedding.
It rejoices like a great athlete eager to run the race.

⁶ The sun rises at one end of the heavens
and follows its course to the other end.
Nothing can hide from its heat.

⁷ The instructions of the LORD are perfect,
reviving the soul.
The decrees of the LORD are trustworthy,
making wise the simple.

⁸ The commandments of the LORD are right,
bringing joy to the heart.
The commands of the LORD are clear,
giving insight for living.

⁹ Reverence for the LORD is pure, lasting forever.
The laws of the LORD are true; each one is fair.

¹⁰ They are more desirable than gold,
even the finest gold.
They are sweeter than honey,
even honey dripping from the comb.

¹¹ They are a warning to your servant,
a great reward for those who obey them.

¹² How can I know all the sins lurking in my heart?
Cleanse me from these hidden faults.

¹³ Keep your servant from deliberate sins!
Don't let them control me.
Then I will be free of guilt
and innocent of great sin.

¹⁴ May the words of my mouth
and the meditation of my heart
be pleasing to you,
O LORD, my rock and my redeemer.

20

For the choir director: A psalm of David.

¹ In times of trouble, may the LORD answer your cry.
May the name of the God of Jacob
keep you safe from all harm.

² May he send you help from his sanctuary
and strengthen you from Jerusalem.

³ May he remember all your gifts
and look favorably on your burnt offerings.
Interlude

⁴ May he grant your heart's desires
and make all your plans succeed.

⁵ May we shout for joy when
we hear of your victory
and raise a victory banner in the name of our God.
May the LORD answer all your prayers.

⁶ Now I know that the LORD rescues his anointed king.
He will answer him from his holy heaven
and rescue him by his great power.

⁷ Some nations boast of their chariots and horses,
but we boast in the name of the LORD our God.

⁸ Those nations will fall down and collapse,
but we will rise up and stand firm.

⁹ Give victory to our king, O LORD!
Answer our cry for help.

RECOGNIZING GOD

PSALM 19:1-6

READ

1. Read Psalm 19:1-6.
2. Look at the image on page 32.
3. If you are near a window, look outside.

REFLECT

1. Read the passage again. Notice the references to nature and creation.
2. Look again at the image.
3. Notice how the smaller photograph repeats the theme of sky, its borders distinct but also creating physically another layer to the sky.
4. How do your current surroundings proclaim the glory of God? Now think back to what you saw outside. How does what you saw also proclaim the glory of God, expanding how you can experience God while also maintaining distinctions?
5. How can our different words of praise mimic creation in its proclamation of God's glory?
6. Read the passage again. Notice the references to humankind.
7. Describe a bridegroom and imagine him in your mind. Holding that image, describe an athlete and imagine her in your mind.

8. How does the diversity of creation reflect God? How does the diversity of human experiences reflect God? Why do we need this?

RESPOND

1. Look again at the image.
2. Read the passage again.
3. Close your eyes and name out loud, if possible, the ways you see God in your surroundings.
4. In your mind's eye, imagine you are staring at yourself in a mirror. Name out loud, if possible, the way you, your body, your culture, and your experiences proclaim the glory of God.
5. Imagine a friend who does not look like you or doesn't share your culture and name out loud, if possible, the way they proclaim the glory of God.

REST

1. Read the passage again.
2. If you are able, go outside or look out a window and take in the view, recognizing God's glory.

21

For the choir director: A psalm of David.

1 How the king rejoices in your strength, O Lord!
He shouts with joy because you give him victory.
2 For you have given him his heart's desire;
you have withheld nothing he requested.
Interlude
3 You welcomed him back
with success and prosperity.
You placed a crown of finest gold on his head.
4 He asked you to preserve his life,
and you granted his request.
The days of his life stretch on forever.
5 Your victory brings him great honor,
and you have clothed him
with splendor and majesty.
6 You have endowed him with eternal blessings
and given him the joy of your presence.
7 For the king trusts in the Lord.
The unfailing love of the Most High will keep

him from stumbling.
8 You will capture all your enemies.
Your strong right hand
will seize all who hate you.
9 You will throw them in a flaming furnace
when you appear.
The Lord will consume them in his anger;
fire will devour them.
10 You will wipe their children
from the face of the earth;
they will never have descendants.
11 Although they plot against you,
their evil schemes will never succeed.
12 For they will turn and run
when they see your arrows aimed at them.
13 Rise up, O Lord, in all your power.
With music and singing
we celebrate your mighty acts.

22

For the choir director: A psalm of David,
to be sung to the tune "Doe of the Dawn."

1 My God, my God,
  why have you abandoned me?
  Why are you so far away when I groan for help?
2 Every day I call to you, my God,
  but you do not answer.
  Every night I lift my voice, but I find no relief.
3 Yet you are holy,
  enthroned on the praises of Israel.
4 Our ancestors trusted in you,
  and you rescued them.
5 They cried out to you and were saved.
  They trusted in you and were never disgraced.
6 But I am a worm and not a man.
  I am scorned and despised by all!
7 Everyone who sees me mocks me.
  They sneer and shake their heads, saying,
8 "Is this the one who relies on the Lord?
  Then let the Lord save him!
  If the Lord loves him so much,
  let the Lord rescue him!"
9 Yet you brought me safely
  from my mother's womb
  and led me to trust you
  at my mother's breast.
10 I was thrust into your arms at my birth.
  You have been my God
  from the moment I was born.
11 Do not stay so far from me,
  for trouble is near,
  and no one else can help me.
12 My enemies surround me like a herd of bulls;
  fierce bulls of Bashan have hemmed me in!
13 Like lions they open their jaws against me,
  roaring and tearing into their prey.
14 My life is poured out like water,
  and all my bones are out of joint.
  My heart is like wax,
  melting within me.
15 My strength has dried up like sunbaked clay.
  My tongue sticks to the roof of my mouth.
  You have laid me in the dust
  and left me for dead.
16 My enemies surround me like a pack of dogs;
  an evil gang closes in on me.

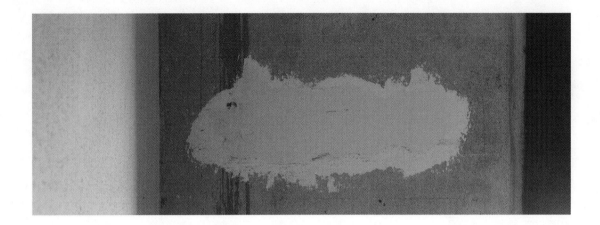

They have pierced my hands and feet.

¹⁷ I can count all my bones.

My enemies stare at me and gloat.

¹⁸ They divide my garments among themselves

and throw dice for my clothing.

¹⁹ O Lᴏʀᴅ, do not stay far away!

You are my strength; come quickly to my aid!

²⁰ Save me from the sword;

spare my precious life from these dogs.

²¹ Snatch me from the lion's jaws

and from the horns of these wild oxen.

²² I will proclaim your name

to my brothers and sisters.

I will praise you among your assembled people.

²³ Praise the Lᴏʀᴅ, all you who fear him!

Honor him, all you descendants of Jacob!

Show him reverence,

all you descendants of Israel!

²⁴ For he has not ignored or

belittled the suffering of the needy.

He has not turned his back on them,

but has listened to their cries for help.

²⁵ I will praise you in the great assembly.

I will fulfill my vows in

the presence of those who worship you.

²⁶ The poor will eat and be satisfied.

All who seek the Lᴏʀᴅ will praise him.

Their hearts will rejoice with everlasting joy.

²⁷ The whole earth will acknowledge

the Lᴏʀᴅ and return to him.

All the families of the nations

will bow down before him.

²⁸ For royal power belongs to the Lᴏʀᴅ.

He rules all the nations.

²⁹ Let the rich of the earth feast and worship.

Bow before him, all who are mortal,

all whose lives will end as dust.

³⁰ Our children will also serve him.

Future generations will hear

about the wonders of the Lord.

³¹ His righteous acts will be

told to those not yet born.

They will hear about

everything he has done.

23

A psalm of David.

1 The Lord is my shepherd;
I have all that I need.

2 He lets me rest in green meadows;
he leads me beside peaceful streams.

3 He renews my strength.
He guides me along right paths,
bringing honor to his name.

4 Even when I walk
through the darkest valley,
I will not be afraid,
for you are close beside me.
Your rod and your staff
protect and comfort me.

5 You prepare a feast for me
in the presence of my enemies.
You honor me by anointing my head with oil.
My cup overflows with blessings.

6 Surely your goodness and
unfailing love will pursue me
all the days of my life,
and I will live in the house of the Lord
forever.

WHAT I NEED

PSALM 23

READ

1. Read Psalm 23.
2. Look at the photograph on page 38. Imagine yourself in the field.

REFLECT

1. Read the passage again, pausing when you come to references to God (second-person pronouns).
2. Who is God in this passage and what does God do?
3. Read the passage, pausing when you come to first-person pronouns.
4. What is happening to you in this passage, and how is God interacting with you?
5. How would you describe the emotional flow of this passage? What is changing in this passage and what remains steady?
6. What ways does God care and provide for our needs in this passage? Physical needs? Emotional needs? Mental needs? Spiritual needs?
7. Look back on the photograph. Imagine yourself in the field. What about the photograph and words reflect peace and abundance? Think about other spaces or places that would make you feel safer and provided for.

RESPOND

1. Think about a place you return to that is your green meadow, a place of renewal, feasting, and love. Describe and name that place and thank God. Write your own psalm patterned after Psalm 23 but set in the place that connects with you and your community.

REST

1. Close your eyes and imagine again being either in the meadow or the space where you feel God's presence the most.
2. Read the passage again. Sit in silence.
3. Read your own psalm, aloud if possible.
4. Savor the feeling of peace as you let the words of David and your own words praise God.

24

A psalm of David.

¹ The earth is the Lord's, and everything in it.
   The world and all its people belong to him.
² For he laid the earth's foundation on the seas
   and built it on the ocean depths.
³ Who may climb the mountain of the Lord?
   Who may stand in his holy place?
⁴ Only those whose hands and hearts are pure,
   who do not worship idols
   and never tell lies.
⁵ They will receive the Lord's blessing
   and have a right relationship
   with God their savior.
⁶ Such people may seek you
   and worship in your presence,
   O God of Jacob.
   Interlude
⁷ Open up, ancient gates!
   Open up, ancient doors,
   and let the King of glory enter.
⁸ Who is the King of glory?
   The Lord, strong and mighty;
   the Lord, invincible in battle.
⁹ Open up, ancient gates!
   Open up, ancient doors,
   and let the King of glory enter.
¹⁰ Who is the King of glory?
   The Lord of Heaven's Armies—
   he is the King of glory.
   Interlude

25

A psalm of David.

¹ O Lord, I give my life to you.

² I trust in you, my God!
  Do not let me be disgraced,
  or let my enemies rejoice in my defeat.

³ No one who trusts in you
  will ever be disgraced,
  but disgrace comes to those who
  try to deceive others.

⁴ Show me the right path, O Lord;
  point out the road for me to follow.

⁵ Lead me by your truth and teach me,
  for you are the God who saves me.
  All day long I put my hope in you.

⁶ Remember, O Lord, your compassion
  and unfailing love,
  which you have shown from long ages past.

⁷ Do not remember
  the rebellious sins of my youth.
  Remember me in the light of
  your unfailing love,
  for you are merciful, O Lord.

⁸ The Lord is good and does what is right;
  he shows the proper path to those who go astray.

⁹ He leads the humble in doing right,
  teaching them his way.

¹⁰ The LORD leads with
unfailing love and faithfulness
all who keep his covenant
and obey his demands.

¹¹ For the honor of your name, O LORD,
forgive my many, many sins.

¹² Who are those who fear the LORD?
He will show them the path they should choose.

¹³ They will live in prosperity,
and their children will inherit the land.

¹⁴ The LORD is a friend to those who fear him.
He teaches them his covenant.

¹⁵ My eyes are always on the LORD,
for he rescues me from
the traps of my enemies.

¹⁶ Turn to me and have mercy,
for I am alone and in deep distress.

¹⁷ My problems go from bad to worse.
Oh, save me from them all!

¹⁸ Feel my pain and see my trouble.
Forgive all my sins.

¹⁹ See how many enemies I have
and how viciously they hate me!

²⁰ Protect me! Rescue my life from them!
Do not let me be disgraced,
for in you I take refuge.

²¹ May integrity and honesty protect me,
for I put my hope in you.

²² O God, ransom Israel
from all its troubles.

26

A psalm of David.

¹ Declare me innocent, O LORD,
for I have acted with integrity;
I have trusted in the LORD without wavering.

² Put me on trial, LORD, and cross-examine me.
Test my motives and my heart.

³ For I am always aware of your unfailing love,
and I have lived according to your truth.

⁴ I do not spend time with liars
or go along with hypocrites.

⁵ I hate the gatherings of those who do evil,
and I refuse to join in with the wicked.

⁶ I wash my hands to declare my innocence.
I come to your altar, O LORD,

⁷ singing a song of thanksgiving
and telling of all your wonders.

⁸ I love your sanctuary, LORD,
the place where your glorious presence dwells.

⁹ Don't let me suffer the fate of sinners.
Don't condemn me along with murderers.

¹⁰ Their hands are dirty with evil schemes,
and they constantly take bribes.

¹¹ But I am not like that; I live with integrity.
So redeem me and show me mercy.

¹² Now I stand on solid ground,
and I will publicly praise the LORD.

27

A psalm of David.

¹ The LORD is my light and my salvation—
so why should I be afraid?
The LORD is my fortress, protecting me from danger,
so why should I tremble?
² When evil people come to devour me,
when my enemies and foes attack me,
they will stumble and fall.
³ Though a mighty army surrounds me,
my heart will not be afraid.
Even if I am attacked,
I will remain confident.
⁴ The one thing I ask of the LORD—
the thing I seek most—
is to live in the house of the LORD
all the days of my life,
delighting in the LORD's perfections
and meditating in his Temple.
⁵ For he will conceal me there when troubles come;
he will hide me in his sanctuary.
He will place me out of reach on a high rock.
⁶ Then I will hold my head high
above my enemies who surround me.
At his sanctuary I will
offer sacrifices with shouts of joy,

singing and praising the LORD with music.
⁷ Hear me as I pray, O LORD.
Be merciful and answer me!
⁸ My heart has heard you say,
"Come and talk with me."
And my heart responds, "LORD, I am coming."
⁹ Do not turn your back on me.
Do not reject your servant in anger.
You have always been my helper.
Don't leave me now; don't abandon me,
O God of my salvation!
¹⁰ Even if my father and mother abandon me,
the LORD will hold me close.
¹¹ Teach me how to live, O LORD.
Lead me along the right path,
for my enemies are waiting for me.
¹² Do not let me fall into their hands.
For they accuse me of things I've never done;
with every breath they threaten me with violence.
¹³ Yet I am confident I will see the LORD's goodness
while I am here in the land of the living.
¹⁴ Wait patiently for the LORD.
Be brave and courageous.
Yes, wait patiently for the LORD.

OPEN FEAR

PSALM 27:1-6

READ

1. Read Psalm 27:1-6.
2. Look at the image on page 47. What do you see?

REFLECT

1. Read the passage slowly. What words or phrases grab your attention? Spend some time considering why those caught your attention.
2. What comes to mind when you think of a fortress? Protection? Sanctuary? What sounds do you hear when you think of meditation? Protection?
3. Look at the image. What feelings does a place like this evoke?
4. Read the passage again, aloud if possible.
5. The promise is that the Lord is your protector. Enemies and attacks don't necessarily disappear. Even when troubles appear, the Lord is present.
6. Look at the image again. What does a wide open space offer in terms of protection and sanctuary? How might God meet you when you feel like you are vulnerable and exposed? How does God's light and salvation fit into and transcend time and space?

RESPOND

1. Read the passage silently. Take a deep breath in-between sentences to help you slow down.
2. Make a physical or mental list of your fears. God will protect you. God knows your fears. Sometimes our own lack of knowledge is an enemy, so take the time to name the things you fear.
3. Make a physical or mental list of how God has protected you in the past, how God has been your light and salvation. Meditate on those things while releasing the list of fears to God, trusting in God's safety and salvation.
4. If you are so led, sing a song of praise.

REST

1. Take three rounds of breath—inhale deeply through your nose; audibly sigh through your mouth with your exhale.
2. Sit in the knowledge and promise that God's protection and salvation are not limited by structures and spaces.

28

A psalm of David.

1 I pray to you, O Lord, my rock.
Do not turn a deaf ear to me.
For if you are silent,
I might as well give up and die.

2 Listen to my prayer for mercy
as I cry out to you for help,
as I lift my hands toward your holy sanctuary.

3 Do not drag me away with the wicked—
with those who do evil—
those who speak friendly words
to their neighbors
while planning evil in their hearts.

4 Give them the punishment they so richly deserve!
Measure it out in proportion to their wickedness.
Pay them back for all their evil deeds!
Give them a taste of what they have done to others.

5 They care nothing for what the Lord has done
or for what his hands have made.
So he will tear them down,
and they will never be rebuilt!

6 Praise the Lord!
For he has heard my cry for mercy.

7 The Lord is my strength and shield.
I trust him with all my heart.
He helps me, and my heart is filled with joy.
I burst out in songs of thanksgiving.

8 The Lord gives his people strength.
He is a safe fortress for his anointed king.

9 Save your people!
Bless Israel, your special possession.
Lead them like a shepherd,
and carry them in your arms forever.

29

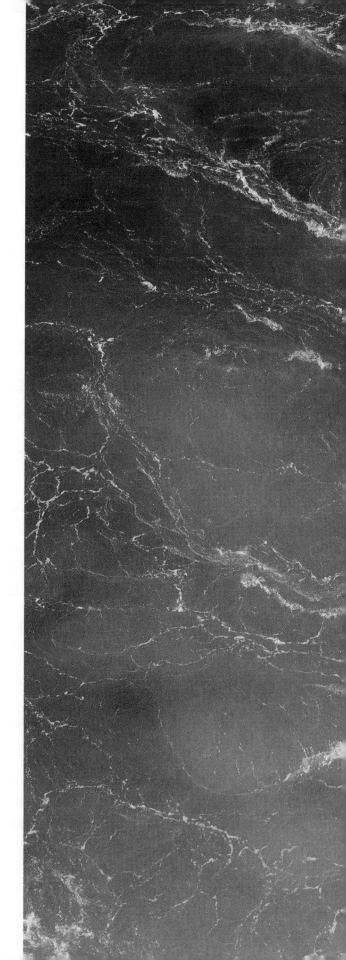

A psalm of David.

¹ Honor the Lord, you heavenly beings;
  honor the Lord for his glory and strength.
² Honor the Lord for
  the glory of his name.
  Worship the Lord
  in the splendor of his holiness.
³ The voice of the Lord
  echoes above the sea.
  The God of glory thunders.
  The Lord thunders over the mighty sea.
⁴ The voice of the Lord is powerful;
  the voice of the Lord is majestic.
⁵ The voice of the Lord
  splits the mighty cedars;
  the Lord shatters the cedars of Lebanon.
⁶ He makes Lebanon's mountains
  skip like a calf;
  he makes Mount Hermon
  leap like a young wild ox.
⁷ The voice of the Lord strikes
  with bolts of lightning.
⁸ The voice of the Lord makes
  the barren wilderness quake;
  the Lord shakes the wilderness of Kadesh.
⁹ The voice of the Lord
  twists mighty oaks
  and strips the forests bare.
  In his Temple everyone shouts, "Glory!"
¹⁰ The Lord rules over the floodwaters.
   The Lord reigns as king forever.
¹¹ The Lord gives his people strength.
   The Lord blesses them with peace.

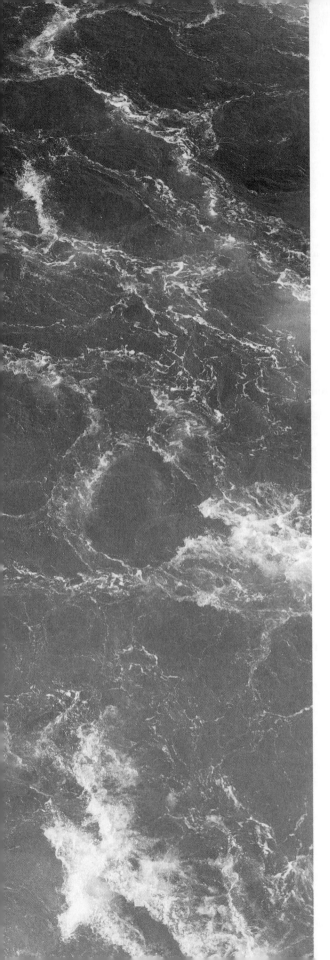

30

*A psalm of David. A song for
the dedication of the Temple.*

¹ I will exalt you, LORD, for you rescued me.
You refused to let my enemies triumph over me.

² O LORD my God, I cried to you for help,
and you restored my health.

³ You brought me up from the grave, O LORD.
You kept me from falling into the pit of death.

⁴ Sing to the LORD, all you godly ones!
Praise his holy name.

⁵ For his anger lasts only a moment,
but his favor lasts a lifetime!
Weeping may last through the night,
but joy comes with the morning.

⁶ When I was prosperous, I said,
"Nothing can stop me now!"

⁷ Your favor, O LORD,
made me as secure as a mountain.
Then you turned away from me,
and I was shattered.

⁸ I cried out to you, O LORD.
I begged the Lord for mercy, saying,

⁹ "What will you gain if I die,
if I sink into the grave?
Can my dust praise you?
Can it tell of your faithfulness?

¹⁰ Hear me, LORD, and have mercy on me.
Help me, O LORD."

¹¹ You have turned my mourning into joyful dancing.
You have taken away my clothes of mourning
and clothed me with joy,

¹² that I might sing praises to you and not be silent.
O LORD my God, I will give you thanks forever!

31

For the choir director: A psalm of David.

1 O LORD, I have come to you for protection;
don't let me be disgraced.
Save me, for you do what is right.

2 Turn your ear to listen to me;
rescue me quickly.
Be my rock of protection,
a fortress where I will be safe.

3 You are my rock and my fortress.
For the honor of your name,
lead me out of this danger.

4 Pull me from the trap my enemies set for me,
for I find protection in you alone.

5 I entrust my spirit into your hand.
Rescue me, LORD, for you are a faithful God.

6 I hate those who worship worthless idols.
I trust in the LORD.

7 I will be glad and rejoice in your unfailing love,
for you have seen my troubles,
and you care about the anguish of my soul.

8 You have not handed me over to my enemies
but have set me in a safe place.

9 Have mercy on me, LORD, for I am in distress.
Tears blur my eyes.
My body and soul are withering away.

10 I am dying from grief;
my years are shortened by sadness.
Sin has drained my strength;
I am wasting away from within.

11 I am scorned by all my enemies
and despised by my neighbors—
even my friends are afraid to come near me.
When they see me on the street,
they run the other way.

12 I am ignored as if I were dead,
as if I were a broken pot.

13 I have heard the many rumors about me,
and I am surrounded by terror.
My enemies conspire against me,
plotting to take my life.

14 But I am trusting you, O LORD,
saying, "You are my God!"

15 My future is in your hands.
Rescue me from those who
hunt me down relentlessly.

16 Let your favor shine on your servant.
In your unfailing love, rescue me.

17 Don't let me be disgraced, O LORD,
for I call out to you for help.
Let the wicked be disgraced;
let them lie silent in the grave.

18 Silence their lying lips—
those proud and arrogant lips
that accuse the godly.

19 How great is the goodness
you have stored up for those who fear you.
You lavish it on those who
come to you for protection,
blessing them before the watching world.

20 You hide them in the shelter of your presence,

safe from those who conspire against them.
You shelter them in your presence,
far from accusing tongues.
²¹ Praise the Lord,
for he has shown me
the wonders of his unfailing love.
He kept me safe when my city was under attack.
²² In panic I cried out,
"I am cut off from the Lord!"
But you heard my cry for mercy
and answered my call for help.
²³ Love the Lord, all you godly ones!
For the Lord protects those
who are loyal to him,
but he harshly punishes the arrogant.
²⁴ So be strong and courageous,
all you who put your hope in the Lord!

32

A psalm of David.

¹ Oh, what joy for those
whose disobedience is forgiven,
whose sin is put out of sight!
² Yes, what joy for those
whose record the Lord has cleared of guilt,
whose lives are lived in complete honesty!
³ When I refused to confess my sin,
my body wasted away,

and I groaned all day long.
⁴ Day and night your hand of
discipline was heavy on me.
My strength evaporated like
water in the summer heat.

Interlude

⁵ Finally, I confessed all my sins to you
and stopped trying to hide my guilt.
I said to myself,
"I will confess my rebellion to the Lord."
And you forgave me! All my guilt is gone.

Interlude

⁶ Therefore, let all the godly
pray to you while there is still time,
that they may not drown in
the floodwaters of judgment.
⁷ For you are my hiding place;
you protect me from trouble.
You surround me with songs of victory.

Interlude

⁸ The Lord says, "I will guide you
along the best pathway for your life.
I will advise you and watch over you.
⁹ Do not be like a senseless horse or mule
that needs a bit and bridle
to keep it under control."
¹⁰ Many sorrows come to the wicked,
but unfailing love surrounds those
who trust the Lord.
¹¹ So rejoice in the Lord and be glad,
all you who obey him!
Shout for joy, all you whose hearts are pure!

33

¹ Let the godly sing for joy to the Lord;
  it is fitting for the pure to praise him.

² Praise the Lord with melodies on the lyre;
  make music for him on the ten-stringed harp.

³ Sing a new song of praise to him;
  play skillfully on the harp, and sing with joy.

⁴ For the word of the Lord holds true,
  and we can trust everything he does.

⁵ He loves whatever is just and good;
  the unfailing love of the Lord fills the earth.

⁶ The Lord merely spoke,
  and the heavens were created.
  He breathed the word,
  and all the stars were born.

⁷ He assigned the sea its boundaries
  and locked the oceans in vast reservoirs.

⁸ Let the whole world fear the Lord,
  and let everyone stand in awe of him.

⁹ For when he spoke, the world began!
  It appeared at his command.

¹⁰ The Lord frustrates the plans of the nations
  and thwarts all their schemes.

¹¹ But the Lord's plans stand firm forever;
  his intentions can never be shaken.

¹² What joy for the nation
  whose God is the Lord,
  whose people he has
  chosen as his inheritance.

¹³ The Lord looks down from heaven
  and sees the whole human race.

¹⁴ From his throne he observes
  all who live on the earth.

¹⁵ He made their hearts,
  so he understands everything they do.

¹⁶ The best-equipped army
  cannot save a king,
  nor is great strength
  enough to save a warrior.

¹⁷ Don't count on your warhorse
  to give you victory—
  for all its strength, it cannot save you.

¹⁸ But the Lord watches over
  those who fear him,
  those who rely on his unfailing love.

¹⁹ He rescues them from death
  and keeps them alive in times of famine.

²⁰ We put our hope in the Lord.
  He is our help and our shield.

²¹ In him our hearts rejoice,
  for we trust in his holy name.

²² Let your unfailing love surround us, Lord,
  for our hope is in you alone.

MADE TO PRAISE

PSALM 33:1-3

READ

1. Read Psalm 33:1-3.
2. Pause.
3. Read the passage again, paying attention to the verbs.
4. Look at the photograph on page 54. How does the woman's expression make you feel?

REFLECT

1. Read the passage, aloud if possible.
2. What does this passage tell you about praise?
3. Look again at the photograph. The woman isn't singing or playing an instrument. What does this image show you about praise expressed through our bodies? What does praising God have to do with our bodies? Our words? Our abilities?
4. How does singing elicit joy? How does music help you praise God?
5. What other ways of self-expression do you find helpful, or perhaps more helpful than singing or music, to praise God?
6. What preconceived notions are you holding onto about what are appropriate and inappropriate expressions of praise and joy?

RESPOND

1. If you are able, stand to read the passage, moving as led to move.
2. Make a list of words and phrases expressing your praise of God. Instead of reading the list out loud, try something just outside of what is comfortable and in your tradition. Perhaps sing or chant the words of praise, move through the words, or create a piece of visual art while meditating on the words of praise.
3. How might God be inviting you to praise with words and your body?

REST

1. Sit down and take some steady breaths, especially if you have been moving physically.
2. Read the passage one last time. Enjoy the freedom to praise God and sing for joy in new ways.

34

A psalm of David, regarding the time he pretended to be insane in front of Abimelech, who sent him away.

1 I will praise the LORD at all times.
I will constantly speak his praises.
2 I will boast only in the LORD;
let all who are helpless take heart.
3 Come, let us tell of the LORD's greatness;
let us exalt his name together.
4 I prayed to the LORD, and he answered me.
He freed me from all my fears.
5 Those who look to him for help
will be radiant with joy;
no shadow of shame will darken their faces.
6 In my desperation I prayed,
and the LORD listened;
he saved me from all my troubles.
7 For the angel of the LORD is a guard;
he surrounds and defends all who fear him.
8 Taste and see that the LORD is good.
Oh, the joys of those who take refuge in him!
9 Fear the LORD, you his godly people,
for those who fear him will have all they need.
10 Even strong young lions sometimes go hungry,
but those who trust in the LORD
will lack no good thing.
11 Come, my children, and listen to me,
and I will teach you to fear the LORD.
12 Does anyone want to live a life
that is long and prosperous?
13 Then keep your tongue from speaking evil
and your lips from telling lies!
14 Turn away from evil and do good.
Search for peace, and work to maintain it.
15 The eyes of the LORD
watch over those who do right;
his ears are open to their cries for help.
16 But the LORD turns his face
against those who do evil;
he will erase their memory from the earth.
17 The LORD hears his people
when they call to him for help.
He rescues them from all their troubles.
18 The LORD is close to the brokenhearted;
he rescues those whose spirits are crushed.
19 The righteous person faces many troubles,
but the LORD comes to the rescue each time.
20 For the LORD protects the bones of the righteous;
not one of them is broken!
21 Calamity will surely destroy the wicked,
and those who hate the righteous will be punished.
22 But the LORD will redeem those who serve him.
No one who takes refuge in him will be condemned.

35

A psalm of David.

¹ O Lord, oppose those who oppose me.
Fight those who fight against me.
² Put on your armor, and take up your shield.
Prepare for battle, and come to my aid.
³ Lift up your spear and javelin
against those who pursue me.
Let me hear you say, "I will give you victory!"
⁴ Bring shame and disgrace
on those trying to kill me;
turn them back and humiliate
those who want to harm me.
⁵ Blow them away like chaff in the wind—
a wind sent by the angel of the Lord.
⁶ Make their path dark and slippery,
with the angel of the Lord pursuing them.
⁷ I did them no wrong, but they laid a trap for me.
I did them no wrong, but they dug a pit to catch me.
⁸ So let sudden ruin come upon them!
Let them be caught in the trap they set for me!
Let them be destroyed in the pit they dug for me.
⁹ Then I will rejoice in the Lord.
I will be glad because he rescues me.
¹⁰ With every bone in my body I will praise him:
"Lord, who can compare with you?
Who else rescues the helpless from the strong?
Who else protects the helpless and poor
from those who rob them?"
¹¹ Malicious witnesses testify against me.
They accuse me of crimes I know nothing about.
¹² They repay me evil for good.
I am sick with despair.
¹³ Yet when they were ill, I grieved for them.
I denied myself by fasting for them,
but my prayers returned unanswered.
¹⁴ I was sad, as though they were my friends or family,
as if I were grieving for my own mother.
¹⁵ But they are glad now that I am in trouble;
they gleefully join together against me.

¹⁶ I am attacked by people I don't even know;
they slander me constantly.
¹⁶ They mock me and call me names; they snarl at me.
¹⁷ How long, O Lord, will you look on and do nothing?
Rescue me from their fierce attacks.
Protect my life from these lions!
¹⁸ Then I will thank you in front of the great assembly.
I will praise you before all the people.
¹⁹ Don't let my treacherous enemies
rejoice over my defeat.
Don't let those who hate me without cause
gloat over my sorrow.
²⁰ They don't talk of peace;
they plot against innocent people
who mind their own business.
²¹ They shout, "Aha! Aha!
With our own eyes we saw him do it!"
²² O Lord, you know all about this.
Do not stay silent.
Do not abandon me now, O Lord.
²³ Wake up! Rise to my defense!
Take up my case, my God and my Lord.
²⁴ Declare me not guilty, O Lord my God,
for you give justice.
Don't let my enemies laugh
about me in my troubles.
²⁵ Don't let them say, "Look, we got what we wanted!
Now we will eat him alive!"
²⁶ May those who rejoice at my troubles
be humiliated and disgraced.
May those who triumph over me
be covered with shame and dishonor.
²⁷ But give great joy to those
who came to my defense.
Let them continually say, "Great is the Lord,
who delights in blessing his servant with peace!"
²⁸ Then I will proclaim your justice,
and I will praise you all day long.

36

*For the choir director: A psalm of David,
the servant of the LORD.*

1 Sin whispers to the wicked,
deep within their hearts.
They have no fear of God at all.

2 In their blind conceit,
they cannot see how wicked they really are.

3 Everything they say is crooked and deceitful.
They refuse to act wisely or do good.

4 They lie awake at night, hatching sinful plots.
Their actions are never good.
They make no attempt to turn from evil.

5 Your unfailing love, O Lord,
is as vast as the heavens;
your faithfulness reaches beyond the clouds.

6 Your righteousness is like the mighty mountains,
your justice like the ocean depths.
You care for people and animals alike, O Lord.

7 How precious is your unfailing love, O God!
All humanity finds shelter
in the shadow of your wings.

8 You feed them from the abundance of
your own house,
letting them drink from your river of delights.

9 For you are the fountain of life,
the light by which we see.

10 Pour out your unfailing love on those who love you;
give justice to those with honest hearts.

11 Don't let the proud trample me
or the wicked push me around.

12 Look! Those who do evil have fallen!
They are thrown down, never to rise again.

37

A psalm of David.

1 Don't worry about the wicked
or envy those who do wrong.

2 For like grass, they soon fade away.
Like spring flowers, they soon wither.

3 Trust in the LORD and do good.
Then you will live safely
in the land and prosper.

4 Take delight in the LORD,
and he will give you your heart's desires.

5 Commit everything you do to the LORD.
Trust him, and he will help you.

6 He will make your innocence
radiate like the dawn,
and the justice of your cause
will shine like the noonday sun.

7 Be still in the presence of the LORD,
and wait patiently for him to act.
Don't worry about evil people who prosper
or fret about their wicked schemes.

8 Stop being angry!
Turn from your rage!
Do not lose your temper—
it only leads to harm.

9 For the wicked will be destroyed,
but those who trust in the LORD
will possess the land.

10 Soon the wicked will disappear.
Though you look for them, they will be gone.

11 The lowly will possess the land
and will live in peace and prosperity.

12 The wicked plot against the godly;

they snarl at them in defiance.

¹³ But the Lord just laughs,
for he sees their day of judgment coming.

¹⁴ The wicked draw their swords
and string their bows
to kill the poor and the oppressed,
to slaughter those who do right.

¹⁵ But their swords will stab their own hearts,
and their bows will be broken.

¹⁶ It is better to be godly and have little
than to be evil and rich.

¹⁷ For the strength of the wicked will be shattered,
but the LORD takes care of the godly.

¹⁸ Day by day the LORD takes care of the innocent,
and they will receive an inheritance
that lasts forever.

¹⁹ They will not be disgraced in hard times;
even in famine they will have
more than enough.

²⁰ But the wicked will die.
The LORD's enemies are like flowers in a field—
they will disappear like smoke.

²¹ The wicked borrow and never repay,
but the godly are generous givers.

²² Those the LORD blesses will possess the land,
but those he curses will die.

²³ The LORD directs the steps of the godly.
He delights in every detail of their lives.

²⁴ Though they stumble, they will never fall,
for the LORD holds them by the hand.

²⁵ Once I was young, and now I am old.
Yet I have never seen the godly abandoned
or their children begging for bread.

²⁶ The godly always give generous loans to others,
and their children are a blessing.

²⁷ Turn from evil and do good,

and you will live in the land forever.

²⁸ For the LORD loves justice,
and he will never abandon the godly.
He will keep them safe forever,
but the children of the wicked will die.

²⁹ The godly will possess the land
and will live there forever.

³⁰ The godly offer good counsel;
they teach right from wrong.

³¹ They have made God's law their own,
so they will never slip from his path.

³² The wicked wait in ambush for the godly,
looking for an excuse to kill them.

³³ But the LORD will not let the wicked succeed
or let the godly be condemned
when they are put on trial.

³⁴ Put your hope in the LORD.
Travel steadily along his path.
He will honor you by giving you the land.
You will see the wicked destroyed.

³⁵ I have seen wicked and ruthless people
flourishing like a tree in its native soil.

³⁶ But when I looked again, they were gone!
Though I searched for them,
I could not find them!

³⁷ Look at those who are honest and good,
for a wonderful future
awaits those who love peace.

³⁸ But the rebellious will be destroyed;
they have no future.

³⁹ The LORD rescues the godly;
he is their fortress in times of trouble.

⁴⁰ The LORD helps them,
rescuing them from the wicked.
He saves them,
and they find shelter in him.

38

A psalm of David, asking God to remember him.

1 O Lord, don't rebuke me in your anger
  or discipline me in your rage!
2 Your arrows have struck deep,
  and your blows are crushing me.
3 Because of your anger, my whole body is sick;
  my health is broken because of my sins.
4 My guilt overwhelms me—
  it is a burden too heavy to bear.
5 My wounds fester and stink
  because of my foolish sins.
6 I am bent over and racked with pain.
  All day long I walk around filled with grief.
7 A raging fever burns within me,
  and my health is broken.
8 I am exhausted and completely crushed.
  My groans come from an anguished heart.
9 You know what I long for, Lord;
  you hear my every sigh.
10 My heart beats wildly, my strength fails,
  and I am going blind.
11 My loved ones and friends stay away,
  fearing my disease.
  Even my own family stands at a distance.

12 Meanwhile, my enemies lay traps to kill me.
  Those who wish me harm make plans to ruin me.
  All day long they plan their treachery.
13 But I am deaf to all their threats.
  I am silent before them as one who cannot speak.
14 I choose to hear nothing,
  and I make no reply.
15 For I am waiting for you, O Lord.
  You must answer for me, O Lord my God.
16 I prayed, "Don't let my enemies gloat over me
  or rejoice at my downfall."
17 I am on the verge of collapse,
  facing constant pain.
18 But I confess my sins;
  I am deeply sorry for what I have done.
19 I have many aggressive enemies;
  they hate me without reason.
20 They repay me evil for good
  and oppose me for pursuing good.
21 Do not abandon me, O Lord.
  Do not stand at a distance, my God.
22 Come quickly to help me,
  O Lord my savior.

39

For Jeduthun, the choir director: A psalm of David.

¹ I said to myself, "I will watch what I do
and not sin in what I say.
I will hold my tongue
when the ungodly are around me."
² But as I stood there in silence—
not even speaking of good things—
the turmoil within me grew worse.
³ The more I thought about it,
the hotter I got,
igniting a fire of words:
⁴ "Lᴏʀᴅ, remind me how brief
my time on earth will be.
Remind me that my days are numbered—
how fleeting my life is.
⁵ You have made my life no longer
than the width of my hand.
My entire lifetime is just a moment to you;
at best, each of us is but a breath."
Interlude
⁶ We are merely moving shadows,
and all our busy rushing ends in nothing.
We heap up wealth,
not knowing who will spend it.
⁷ And so, Lord, where do I put my hope?
My only hope is in you.
⁸ Rescue me from my rebellion.
Do not let fools mock me.
⁹ I am silent before you; I won't say a word,
for my punishment is from you.
¹⁰ But please stop striking me!
I am exhausted by the blows from your hand.
¹¹ When you discipline us for our sins,
you consume like a moth
what is precious to us.
Each of us is but a breath.
Interlude
¹² Hear my prayer, O Lᴏʀᴅ!
Listen to my cries for help!
Don't ignore my tears.
For I am your guest—
a traveler passing through,
as my ancestors were before me.
¹³ Leave me alone so I can smile again
before I am gone and exist no more.

40

For the choir director: A psalm of David.

¹ I waited patiently for the LORD to help me,
and he turned to me and heard my cry.

² He lifted me out of the pit of despair,
out of the mud and the mire.
He set my feet on solid ground
and steadied me as I walked along.

³ He has given me a new song to sing,
a hymn of praise to our God.
Many will see what he has done and be amazed.
They will put their trust in the LORD.

⁴ Oh, the joys of those who trust the LORD,
who have no confidence in the proud
or in those who worship idols.

⁵ O LORD my God,
you have performed many wonders for us.
Your plans for us are too numerous to list.
You have no equal.
If I tried to recite all your wonderful deeds,
I would never come to the end of them.

⁶ You take no delight in sacrifices or offerings.
Now that you have made me listen,
I finally understand—
you don't require burnt offerings or sin offerings.

⁷ Then I said, "Look, I have come.
As is written about me in the Scriptures:

⁸ I take joy in doing your will, my God,
for your instructions are written on my heart."

⁹ I have told all your people about your justice.
I have not been afraid to speak out,
as you, O LORD, well know.

¹⁰ I have not kept the good news of your justice
hidden in my heart;
I have talked about
your faithfulness and saving power.
I have told everyone in the great assembly
of your unfailing love and faithfulness.

¹¹ LORD, don't hold back
your tender mercies from me.
Let your unfailing love
and faithfulness always protect me.

¹² For troubles surround me—
too many to count!
My sins pile up so high
I can't see my way out.
They outnumber the hairs on my head.
I have lost all courage.

¹³ Please, LORD, rescue me!
Come quickly, LORD, and help me.

¹⁴ May those who try to destroy me
be humiliated and put to shame.
May those who take delight in my trouble
be turned back in disgrace.

¹⁵ Let them be horrified by their shame,
for they said, "Aha! We've got him now!"

¹⁶ But may all who search for you
be filled with joy and gladness in you.
May those who love your salvation
repeatedly shout, "The LORD is great!"

¹⁷ As for me, since I am poor and needy,
let the Lord keep me in his thoughts.
You are my helper and my savior.
O my God, do not delay.

FIND THE WORDS

PSALM 40:8-10

READ

1. Read Psalm 40:8-10.
2. Look at the photograph on page 69 and, if possible, write down what you see and what you can't see.

REFLECT

1. Look at the photograph. How does the fog make you feel? If you've driven through or walked through fog, what did that experience feel like? What did you have to do to make it through safely?
2. Read the passage again, aloud if possible. Pause at the end of each sentence.
3. Think of a recent decision you made. How did you discern God's will in that particular decision? What instructions has God written on your heart?
4. Often we talk about discerning God's will as if it is hidden from us. In this passage, the author emphasizes he has not hidden the good news of God's faithfulness from others. How have you hidden God's faithfulness from yourself and others? How might you be afraid to speak out?
5. Look at the photograph. Consider what kind of photograph of God you are showing and sharing with others.

RESPOND

1. Think about one person with whom you are being invited to have an intentional spiritual conversation. Imagine how that conversation will go, and invite the Holy Spirit to reveal the instructions already written on your heart.

REST

1. Look at the photograph again, imagining what is beyond the fog.
2. Read the passage again. Place one hand on your heart and the other open and outstretched as if you are receiving God's peace and instruction and inviting someone else to join you.
3. Inhale. Exhale.

41

For the choir director: A psalm of David.

¹ Oh, the joys of those who are kind to the poor!
   The LORD rescues them when they are in trouble.
² The LORD protects them
   and keeps them alive.
   He gives them prosperity in the land
   and rescues them from their enemies.
³ The LORD nurses them when they are sick
   and restores them to health.
⁴ "O LORD," I prayed, "have mercy on me.
   Heal me, for I have sinned against you."
⁵ But my enemies say nothing but evil about me.
   "How soon will he die and be forgotten?" they ask.
⁶ They visit me as if they were my friends,
   but all the while they gather gossip,
   and when they leave, they spread it everywhere.
⁷ All who hate me whisper about me,
   imagining the worst.
⁸ "He has some fatal disease," they say.
   "He will never get out of that bed!"
⁹ Even my best friend, the one I trusted completely,
   the one who shared my food, has turned against me.
¹⁰ LORD, have mercy on me.
   Make me well again, so I can pay them back!
¹¹ I know you are pleased with me,
   for you have not let my enemies triumph over me.
¹² You have preserved my life because I am innocent;
   you have brought me into your presence forever.
¹³ Praise the LORD, the God of Israel,
   who lives from everlasting to everlasting.
   Amen and amen!

II.

42

*For the choir director: A psalm of
the descendants of Korah.*

1 As the deer longs for streams of water,
so I long for you, O God.
2 I thirst for God, the living God.
When can I go and stand before him?
3 Day and night I have only tears for food,
while my enemies continually taunt me, saying,
"Where is this God of yours?"
4 My heart is breaking
as I remember how it used to be:
I walked among the crowds of worshipers,
leading a great procession to the house of God,
singing for joy and giving thanks
amid the sound of a great celebration!
5 Why am I discouraged?
Why is my heart so sad?
I will put my hope in God!
I will praise him again—
my Savior and 6 my God!
Now I am deeply discouraged,
but I will remember you—

even from distant Mount Hermon,
the source of the Jordan,
from the land of Mount Mizar.
7 I hear the tumult of the raging seas
as your waves and surging tides sweep over me.
8 But each day the LORD pours
his unfailing love upon me,
and through each night I sing his songs,
praying to God who gives me life.
9 "O God my rock," I cry,
"Why have you forgotten me?
Why must I wander around in grief,
oppressed by my enemies?"
10 Their taunts break my bones.
They scoff, "Where is this God of yours?"
11 Why am I discouraged?
Why is my heart so sad?
I will put my hope in God!
I will praise him again—
my Savior and my God!

43

[1] Declare me innocent, O God!
Defend me against these ungodly people.
Rescue me from these unjust liars.
[2] For you are God, my only safe haven.
Why have you tossed me aside?
Why must I wander around in grief,
oppressed by my enemies?
[3] Send out your light and your truth;
let them guide me.
Let them lead me to your holy mountain,
to the place where you live.
[4] There I will go to the altar of God,
to God—the source of all my joy.
I will praise you with my harp,
O God, my God!
[5] Why am I discouraged?
Why is my heart so sad?
I will put my hope in God!
I will praise him again—
my Savior and my God!

44

*For the choir director: A psalm of
the descendants of Korah.*

1 O God, we have heard it with our own ears—
our ancestors have told us
of all you did in their day, in days long ago:

2 You drove out the pagan nations by your power
and gave all the land to our ancestors.
You crushed their enemies
and set our ancestors free.

3 They did not conquer the land with their swords;
it was not their own strong arm
that gave them victory.
It was your right hand and strong arm
and the blinding light
from your face that helped them,
for you loved them.

4 You are my King and my God.
You command victories for Israel.

5 Only by your power can we push back our enemies;
only in your name can we trample our foes.

6 I do not trust in my bow;
I do not count on my sword to save me.

7 You are the one who gives us
victory over our enemies;
you disgrace those who hate us.

8 O God, we give glory to you all day long
and constantly praise your name.
Interlude

9 But now you have tossed us aside in dishonor.
You no longer lead our armies to battle.

10 You make us retreat from our enemies
and allow those who hate us to plunder our land.

11 You have butchered us like sheep
and scattered us among the nations.

12 You sold your precious people for a pittance,
making nothing on the sale.

13 You let our neighbors mock us.
We are an object of scorn
and derision to those around us.

14 You have made us the butt of their jokes;
they shake their heads at us in scorn.

15 We can't escape the constant humiliation;
shame is written across our faces.

16 All we hear are the taunts of our mockers.
All we see are our vengeful enemies.

17 All this has happened though we have not forgotten you.
We have not violated your covenant.

18 Our hearts have not deserted you.
We have not strayed from your path.

19 Yet you have crushed us in the jackal's desert home.
You have covered us with darkness and death.

20 If we had forgotten the name of our God
or spread our hands in prayer to foreign gods,

21 God would surely have known it,
for he knows the secrets of every heart.

22 But for your sake we are killed every day;
we are being slaughtered like sheep.

23 Wake up, O Lord! Why do you sleep?
Get up! Do not reject us forever.

24 Why do you look the other way?
Why do you ignore our suffering and oppression?

25 We collapse in the dust, lying face down in the dirt.

26 Rise up! Help us!
Ransom us because of your unfailing love.

45

*For the choir director: A love song to be sung to the
tune "Lilies." A psalm of the descendants of Korah.*

¹ Beautiful words stir my heart.
I will recite a lovely poem about the king,
for my tongue is like the pen of a skillful poet.

² You are the most handsome of all.
Gracious words stream from your lips.
God himself has blessed you forever.

³ Put on your sword, O mighty warrior!
You are so glorious, so majestic!

⁴ In your majesty, ride out to victory,
defending truth, humility, and justice.
Go forth to perform awe-inspiring deeds!

⁵ Your arrows are sharp,
piercing your enemies' hearts.
The nations fall beneath your feet.

⁶ Your throne, O God, endures forever and ever.
You rule with a scepter of justice.

⁷ You love justice and hate evil.
Therefore God, your God, has anointed you,
pouring out the oil of joy on you
more than on anyone else.

⁸ Myrrh, aloes, and cassia perfume your robes.
In ivory palaces the music of strings entertains you.

⁹ Kings' daughters are among your noble women.
At your right side stands the queen,
wearing jewelry of finest gold from Ophir!

¹⁰ Listen to me, O royal daughter;
take to heart what I say.
Forget your people and your family far away.

¹¹ For your royal husband delights in your beauty;
honor him, for he is your lord.

¹² The princess of Tyre will shower you with gifts.
The wealthy will beg your favor.

¹³ The bride, a princess, looks glorious
in her golden gown.

¹⁴ In her beautiful robes, she is led to the king,
accompanied by her bridesmaids.

¹⁵ What a joyful and enthusiastic procession
as they enter the king's palace!

¹⁶ Your sons will become kings like their father.
You will make them rulers over many lands.

¹⁷ I will bring honor to your name
in every generation.
Therefore, the nations will
praise you forever and ever.

46

For the choir director: A song of the descendants of Korah, to be sung by soprano voices.

1 God is our refuge and strength,
always ready to help in times of trouble.

2 So we will not fear when earthquakes come
and the mountains crumble into the sea.

3 Let the oceans roar and foam.
Let the mountains tremble
as the waters surge!
Interlude

4 A river brings joy to the city of our God,
the sacred home of the Most High.

5 God dwells in that city;
it cannot be destroyed.
From the very break of day,
God will protect it.

6 The nations are in chaos,
and their kingdoms crumble!
God's voice thunders,
and the earth melts!

7 The Lord of Heaven's Armies
is here among us;
the God of Israel is our fortress.
Interlude

8 Come, see the glorious works of the Lord:
See how he brings destruction upon the world.

9 He causes wars to end throughout the earth.
He breaks the bow and snaps the spear;
he burns the shields with fire.

10 "Be still, and know that I am God!
I will be honored by every nation.
I will be honored throughout the world."

11 The Lord of Heaven's Armies
is here among us;
the God of Israel is our fortress.
Interlude

47

For the choir director: A psalm of the descendants of Korah.

1 Come, everyone! Clap your hands!
Shout to God with joyful praise!

2 For the Lord Most High is awesome.
He is the great King of all the earth.

3 He subdues the nations before us,
putting our enemies beneath our feet.

4 He chose the Promised Land as our inheritance,
the proud possession of Jacob's descendants,
whom he loves.
Interlude

5 God has ascended with a mighty shout.
The Lord has ascended with trumpets blaring.

6 Sing praises to God, sing praises;
sing praises to our King, sing praises!

7 For God is the King over all the earth.
Praise him with a psalm.

8 God reigns above the nations,
sitting on his holy throne.

9 The rulers of the world have gathered together
with the people of the God of Abraham.
For all the kings of the earth belong to God.
He is highly honored everywhere.

MOVE TO GOD

PSALM 47

READ

1. Read Psalm 47.
2. Look at the photograph on page 81.

REFLECT

1. As you are able, stand and read the passage aloud.
2. Look again at the photo. How does the woman's pose make you feel? What do you notice about her? About the scene?
3. Read the passage again. Notice what stands out to you. What words (or phrase) resonate with you? How do you feel when you read the verse encouraging you to clap? To shout? To sing? To praise?
4. How comfortable are you with moving physically in response to God? When you think about praising God, is your response physical (a movement of your body) or in your mind (a movement of thoughts)? How has singing, clapping, or shouting been a part of your personal or corporate worship experience?

RESPOND

1. The psalms are a collection of poems meant to be sung. Think about that as you read the passage again, aloud if possible.
2. Write or speak your own psalm, listing praises and the characteristics of God. Bring movement into your reading or the silent recitation of your psalm because we are embodied, able to bring our embodied selves into praise and worship.

REST

1. Look at the photograph and imagine the woman moving from praise and singing into a posture of rest.
2. If you aren't already seated, find a comfortable seated posture. Read the passage again.
3. Let the movement and praise settle into silence.

48

A song. A psalm of the descendants of Korah.

¹ How great is the LORD,
  how deserving of praise,
  in the city of our God,
  which sits on his holy mountain!

² It is high and magnificent;
  the whole earth rejoices to see it!
  Mount Zion, the holy mountain,
  is the city of the great King!

³ God himself is in Jerusalem's towers,
  revealing himself as its defender.

⁴ The kings of the earth joined forces
  and advanced against the city.

⁵ But when they saw it, they were stunned;
  they were terrified and ran away.

⁶ They were gripped with terror
  and writhed in pain like a woman in labor.

⁷ You destroyed them like
  the mighty ships of Tarshish
  shattered by a powerful east wind.

⁸ We had heard of the city's glory,
  but now we have seen it ourselves—
  the city of the LORD of Heaven's Armies.
  It is the city of our God;
  he will make it safe forever.

  Interlude

⁹ O God, we meditate on your unfailing love
  as we worship in your Temple.

¹⁰ As your name deserves, O God,
  you will be praised to the ends of the earth.
  Your strong right hand is filled with victory.

¹¹ Let the people on Mount Zion rejoice.
  Let all the towns of Judah be glad
  because of your justice.

¹² Go, inspect the city of Jerusalem.
  Walk around and count the many towers.

¹³ Take note of the fortified walls,
  and tour all the citadels,
  that you may describe them
  to future generations.

¹⁴ For that is what God is like.
  He is our God forever and ever,
  and he will guide us until we die.

49

For the choir director: A psalm of
the descendants of Korah.

¹ Listen to this, all you people!
  Pay attention, everyone in the world!
² High and low, rich and poor—listen!
³ For my words are wise,
  and my thoughts are filled with insight.
⁴ I listen carefully to many proverbs
  and solve riddles with inspiration from a harp.
⁵ Why should I fear when trouble comes,
  when enemies surround me?
⁶ They trust in their wealth
  and boast of great riches.
⁷ Yet they cannot redeem themselves from death
  by paying a ransom to God.
⁸ Redemption does not come so easily,
  for no one can ever pay enough
⁹ to live forever and never see the grave.
¹⁰ Those who are wise must finally die,
  just like the foolish and senseless,
  leaving all their wealth behind.
¹¹ The grave is their eternal home,
  where they will stay forever.
  They may name their estates after themselves,
¹² but their fame will not last.
  They will die, just like animals.
¹³ This is the fate of fools,
  though they are remembered as being wise.
  Interlude
¹⁴ Like sheep, they are led to the grave,
  where death will be their shepherd.
  In the morning the godly will rule over them.
  Their bodies will rot in the grave,
  far from their grand estates.
¹⁵ But as for me, God will redeem my life.
  He will snatch me from the power of the grave.
  Interlude
¹⁶ So don't be dismayed when the wicked grow rich
  and their homes become ever more splendid.
¹⁷ For when they die, they take nothing with them.
  Their wealth will not follow them into the grave.
¹⁸ In this life they consider themselves fortunate
  and are applauded for their success.
¹⁹ But they will die like all before them
  and never again see the light of day.
²⁰ People who boast of their wealth don't understand;
  they will die, just like animals.

50

A psalm of Asaph.

¹ The LORD, the Mighty One, is God,
  and he has spoken;
  he has summoned all humanity
  from where the sun rises to where it sets.

² From Mount Zion,

the perfection of beauty,

God shines in glorious radiance.

³ Our God approaches,

and he is not silent.

Fire devours everything in his way,

and a great storm rages around him.

⁴ He calls on the heavens above and earth below

to witness the judgment of his people.

⁵ "Bring my faithful people to me—

those who made a covenant with me

by giving sacrifices."

⁶ Then let the heavens proclaim his justice,

for God himself will be the judge.

Interlude

⁷ "O my people, listen as I speak.

Here are my charges against you, O Israel:

I am God, your God!

⁸ I have no complaint about your sacrifices

or the burnt offerings you constantly offer.

⁹ But I do not need the bulls from your barns

or the goats from your pens.

¹⁰ For all the animals of the forest are mine,

and I own the cattle on a thousand hills.

¹¹ I know every bird on the mountains,

and all the animals of the field are mine.

¹² If I were hungry, I would not tell you,

for all the world is mine and everything in it.

¹³ Do I eat the meat of bulls?

Do I drink the blood of goats?

¹⁴ Make thankfulness your sacrifice to God,

and keep the vows you made

to the Most High.

¹⁵ Then call on me when you are in trouble,

and I will rescue you,

and you will give me glory."

¹⁶ But God says to the wicked:

"Why bother reciting my decrees

and pretending to obey my covenant?

¹⁷ For you refuse my discipline

and treat my words like trash.

¹⁸ When you see thieves, you approve of them,

and you spend your time with adulterers.

¹⁹ Your mouth is filled with wickedness,

and your tongue is full of lies.

²⁰ You sit around and slander your brother—

your own mother's son.

²¹ While you did all this, I remained silent,

and you thought I didn't care.

But now I will rebuke you,

listing all my charges against you.

²² Repent, all of you who forget me,

or I will tear you apart,

and no one will help you.

²³ But giving thanks is a sacrifice

that truly honors me.

If you keep to my path,

I will reveal to you the salvation of God."

51

*For the choir director: A psalm of David, regarding the
time Nathan the prophet came to him after David
had committed adultery with Bathsheba.*

1 Have mercy on me, O God,
   because of your unfailing love.
   Because of your great compassion,
   blot out the stain of my sins.
2 Wash me clean from my guilt.
   Purify me from my sin.
3 For I recognize my rebellion;
   it haunts me day and night.
4 Against you, and you alone, have I sinned;
   I have done what is evil in your sight.
   You will be proved right in what you say,
   and your judgment against me is just.
5 For I was born a sinner—
   yes, from the moment my mother conceived me.
6 But you desire honesty from the womb,
   teaching me wisdom even there.
7 Purify me from my sins, and I will be clean;
   wash me, and I will be whiter than snow.
8 Oh, give me back my joy again;
   you have broken me—
   now let me rejoice.
9 Don't keep looking at my sins.
   Remove the stain of my guilt.

10 Create in me a clean heart, O God.
    Renew a loyal spirit within me.
11 Do not banish me from your presence,
    and don't take your Holy Spirit from me.
12 Restore to me the joy of your salvation,
    and make me willing to obey you.
13 Then I will teach your ways to rebels,
    and they will return to you.
14 Forgive me for shedding blood, O God who saves;
    then I will joyfully sing of your forgiveness.
15 Unseal my lips, O Lord,
    that my mouth may praise you.
16 You do not desire a sacrifice, or I would offer one.
    You do not want a burnt offering.
17 The sacrifice you desire is a broken spirit.
    You will not reject a broken
    and repentant heart, O God.
18 Look with favor on Zion and help her;
    rebuild the walls of Jerusalem.
19 Then you will be pleased with
    sacrifices offered in the right spirit—
    with burnt offerings and whole burnt offerings.
    Then bulls will again be sacrificed on your altar.

MAKE YOUR REQUEST KNOWN

PSALM 51:10-17

READ

1. Read Psalm 51:10-17.
2. Look at the photograph on page 87. Notice the details of the photograph.

REFLECT

1. Read the passage again. Notice what stands out to you. What words or phrases capture your imagination? What do those words mean to you? What experiences do they bring back to your consciousness?
2. Look at the photograph. Notice the person is walking toward the tree. How does the person's movement toward the tree make you feel? How might that be an invitation from God?
3. There are a series of requests made to God. Read the passage again, pausing after each request.

RESPOND

1. Is there a request in this passage you resonate with? Talk with God about your desire for renewal, joy, or forgiveness. Ask God to unseal your lips.
2. Look at the photograph. Imagine God is the tree. Where are you in relationship to God? As you are able, place a finger on the spot where you are in the photo. Are you walking toward God? Standing in place? Moving away? Silent?
3. Describe to God where you are in relationship to joy and praise, your connection to the Holy Spirit, and then, if you have a desire to shift, make that request to God.

REST

1. Look at the photograph.
2. Take comfort, joy, and peace that God does not move away from you. God does not leave. You may be far away. You may turn away. You may close your eyes or your vision may change, but God is there.
3. Read the passage again.
4. Pause.
5. Inhale. Exhale.

52

1 Why do you boast about your crimes, great warrior?
Don't you realize God's justice continues forever?
2 All day long you plot destruction.
Your tongue cuts like a sharp razor;
you're an expert at telling lies.
3 You love evil more than good
and lies more than truth.

Interlude

4 You love to destroy others
with your words,
you liar!
5 But God will strike you down
once and for all.
He will pull you from your home
and uproot you from the land of the living.

Interlude

6 The righteous will see it and be amazed.
They will laugh and say,
7 "Look what happens to mighty warriors
who do not trust in God.
They trust their wealth instead
and grow more and more bold
in their wickedness."
8 But I am like an olive tree,
thriving in the house of God.
I will always trust in God's unfailing love.
9 I will praise you forever, O God,
for what you have done.
I will trust in your good name
in the presence of your faithful people.

53

For the choir director: A meditation; a psalm of David.

1 Only fools say in their hearts,
"There is no God."
They are corrupt, and their actions are evil;
not one of them does good!

2 God looks down from heaven
on the entire human race;
he looks to see if anyone is truly wise,
if anyone seeks God.

3 But no, all have turned away;
all have become corrupt.
No one does good,
not a single one!

4 Will those who do evil never learn?
They eat up my people like bread
and wouldn't think of praying to God.

5 Terror will grip them,
terror like they have never known before.
God will scatter the bones of your enemies.
You will put them to shame,
for God has rejected them.

6 Who will come from Mount Zion to rescue Israel?
When God restores his people,
Jacob will shout with joy, and Israel will rejoice.

54

For the choir director: A psalm of David, regarding the time the Ziphites came and said to Saul, "We know where David is hiding." To be accompanied by stringed instruments.

1 Come with great power, O God, and rescue me!
Defend me with your might.

2 Listen to my prayer, O God.
Pay attention to my plea.

3 For strangers are attacking me;
violent people are trying to kill me.
They care nothing for God.
Interlude

4 But God is my helper. The Lord keeps me alive!

5 May the evil plans of my enemies be turned
against them.
Do as you promised and put an end to them.

6 I will sacrifice a voluntary offering to you;
I will praise your name, O LORD,
for it is good.

7 For you have rescued me from my troubles
and helped me to triumph over my enemies.

55

*For the choir director: A psalm of David,
to be accompanied by stringed instruments.*

1 Listen to my prayer, O God.
Do not ignore my cry for help!

2 Please listen and answer me,
for I am overwhelmed by my troubles.

3 My enemies shout at me,
making loud and wicked threats.
They bring trouble on me
and angrily hunt me down.

4 My heart pounds in my chest.
The terror of death assaults me.

5 Fear and trembling overwhelm me,
and I can't stop shaking.

6 Oh, that I had wings like a dove;
then I would fly away and rest!

7 I would fly far away
to the quiet of the wilderness.

8 How quickly I would escape—
    far from this wild storm of hatred.
9 Confuse them, Lord,
    and frustrate their plans,
    for I see violence and conflict in the city.
10 Its walls are patrolled
    day and night against invaders,
    but the real danger is
    wickedness within the city.
11 Everything is falling apart;
    threats and cheating
    are rampant in the streets.
12 It is not an enemy who taunts me—
    I could bear that.
    It is not my foes who so arrogantly insult me—
    I could have hidden from them.
13 Instead, it is you—my equal,
    my companion and close friend.
14 What good fellowship we once enjoyed
    as we walked together to the house of God.
15 Let death stalk my enemies;
    let the grave swallow them alive,
    for evil makes its home within them.
16 But I will call on God,
    and the LORD will rescue me.
17 Morning, noon, and night
    I cry out in my distress,
    and the LORD hears my voice.
18 He ransoms me and keeps me safe
    from the battle waged against me,
    though many still oppose me.
19 God, who has ruled forever,
    will hear me and humble them.
    Interlude
    For my enemies refuse
    to change their ways;
    they do not fear God.

20 As for my companion,
    he betrayed his friends;
    he broke his promises.
21 His words are as smooth as butter,
    but in his heart is war.
    His words are as soothing as lotion,
    but underneath are daggers!
22 Give your burdens to the LORD,
    and he will take care of you.
    He will not permit the godly to slip and fall.
23 But you, O God,
    will send the wicked
    down to the pit of destruction.
    Murderers and liars will die young,
    but I am trusting you to save me.

56

For the choir director: A psalm of David, regarding the time the Philistines seized him in Gath. To be sung to the tune "Dove on Distant Oaks."

1 O God, have mercy on me,

for people are hounding me.

My foes attack me all day long.

2 I am constantly hounded by those who slander me,

and many are boldly attacking me.

3 But when I am afraid,

I will put my trust in you.

4 I praise God for what he has promised.

I trust in God, so why should I be afraid?

What can mere mortals do to me?

5 They are always twisting what I say;

they spend their days plotting to harm me.

6 They come together to spy on me—

watching my every step, eager to kill me.

7 Don't let them get away with their wickedness;

in your anger, O God, bring them down.

8 You keep track of all my sorrows.

You have collected all my tears in your bottle.

You have recorded each one in your book.

9 My enemies will retreat when I call to you for help.

This I know: God is on my side!

10 I praise God for what he has promised;

yes, I praise the Lord for what he has promised.

11 I trust in God, so why should I be afraid?

What can mere mortals do to me?

12 I will fulfill my vows to you, O God,

and will offer a sacrifice of thanks for your help.

13 For you have rescued me from death;

you have kept my feet from slipping.

So now I can walk in your presence, O God,

in your life-giving light.

Your faithfulness reaches to the clouds.

¹¹ Be exalted, O God, above the highest heavens.
May your glory shine over all the earth.

57

For the choir director: A psalm of David, regarding the time he fled from Saul and went into the cave. To be sung to the tune "Do Not Destroy!"

¹ Have mercy on me, O God, have mercy!
I look to you for protection.
I will hide beneath the shadow of your wings
until the danger passes by.

² I cry out to God Most High,
to God who will fulfill his purpose for me.

³ He will send help from heaven to rescue me,
disgracing those who hound me.
Interlude
My God will send forth
his unfailing love and faithfulness.

⁴ I am surrounded by fierce lions
who greedily devour human prey—
whose teeth pierce like spears and arrows,
and whose tongues cut like swords.

⁵ Be exalted, O God, above the highest heavens!
May your glory shine over all the earth.

⁶ My enemies have set a trap for me.
I am weary from distress.
They have dug a deep pit in my path,
but they themselves have fallen into it.
Interlude

⁷ My heart is confident in you, O God;
my heart is confident.
No wonder I can sing your praises!

⁸ Wake up, my heart! Wake up, O lyre and harp!
I will wake the dawn with my song.

⁹ I will thank you, Lord, among all the people.
I will sing your praises among the nations.

¹⁰ For your unfailing love
is as high as the heavens.

58

For the choir director: A psalm of David, to be sung to the tune "Do Not Destroy!"

¹ Justice—do you rulers know
the meaning of the word?
Do you judge the people fairly?

² No! You plot injustice in your hearts.
You spread violence throughout the land.

³ These wicked people are born sinners;
even from birth they have
lied and gone their own way.

⁴ They spit venom like deadly snakes;
they are like cobras that refuse to listen,

⁵ ignoring the tunes of the snake charmers,
no matter how skillfully they play.

⁶ Break off their fangs, O God!
Smash the jaws of these lions, O LORD!

⁷ May they disappear like water into thirsty ground.
Make their weapons useless in their hands.

⁸ May they be like snails that dissolve into slime,
like a stillborn child who will never see the sun.

⁹ God will sweep them away, both young and old,
faster than a pot heats over burning thorns.

¹⁰ The godly will rejoice when
they see injustice avenged.
They will wash their feet in the blood of the wicked.

¹¹ Then at last everyone will say,
"There truly is a reward for those who live for God;
surely there is a God who
judges justly here on earth."

59

For the choir director: A psalm of David, regarding the time Saul sent soldiers to watch David's house in order to kill him. To be sung to the tune "Do Not Destroy!"

¹ Rescue me from my enemies, O God.
Protect me from those
who have come to destroy me.
² Rescue me from these criminals;

save me from these murderers.
³ They have set an ambush for me.
Fierce enemies are out there waiting, LORD,
though I have not sinned or offended them.
⁴ I have done nothing wrong,
yet they prepare to attack me.
Wake up! See what is happening and help me!
⁵ O LORD God of Heaven's Armies,
the God of Israel,
wake up and punish those hostile nations.
Show no mercy to wicked traitors.

Interlude

6 They come out at night,
snarling like vicious dogs
as they prowl the streets.

7 Listen to the filth that comes from their mouths;
their words cut like swords.
"After all, who can hear us?" they sneer.

8 But Lord, you laugh at them.
You scoff at all the hostile nations.

9 You are my strength; I wait for you to rescue me,
for you, O God, are my fortress.

10 In his unfailing love, my God will stand with me.
He will let me look down in triumph
on all my enemies.

11 Don't kill them, for my people
soon forget such lessons;
stagger them with your power,
and bring them to their knees,
O Lord our shield.

12 Because of the sinful things they say,
because of the evil that is on their lips,
let them be captured by their pride,
their curses, and their lies.

13 Destroy them in your anger!
Wipe them out completely!
Then the whole world will know
that God reigns in Israel.
Interlude

14 My enemies come out at night,
snarling like vicious dogs as they prowl the streets.

15 They scavenge for food
but go to sleep unsatisfied.

16 But as for me, I will sing about your power.
Each morning I will sing with joy
about your unfailing love.
For you have been my refuge,
a place of safety when I am in distress.

17 O my Strength, to you I sing praises,
for you, O God, are my refuge,
the God who shows me unfailing love.

60

*For the choir director: A psalm of David useful for
teaching, regarding the time David fought Aram-
naharaim and Aram-zobah, and Joab returned and killed
12,000 Edomites in the Valley of Salt. To be sung to the
tune "Lily of the Testimony."*

1 You have rejected us, O God,
and broken our defenses.
You have been angry with us;
now restore us to your favor.

2 You have shaken our land and split it open.
Seal the cracks, for the land trembles.

3 You have been very hard on us,
making us drink wine that sent us reeling.

4 But you have raised a banner
for those who fear you—
a rallying point in the face of attack.
Interlude

5 Now rescue your beloved people.
Answer and save us by your power.

6 God has promised this by his holiness:
"I will divide up Shechem with joy.
I will measure out the valley of Succoth.

7 Gilead is mine, and Manasseh, too.
Ephraim, my helmet, will produce my warriors,
and Judah, my scepter, will produce my kings.

8 But Moab, my washbasin, will become my servant,
and I will wipe my feet on Edom
and shout in triumph over Philistia."

9 Who will bring me into the fortified city?
Who will bring me victory over Edom?

10 Have you rejected us, O God?
Will you no longer march with our armies?

11 Oh, please help us against our enemies,
for all human help is useless.

12 With God's help we will do mighty things,
for he will trample down our foes.

WHOSE ENEMY?

PSALM 59:9-17

READ

1. Read Psalm 59:9-13 and then pause. Continue reading Psalm 59:14-17.
2. Look at the photograph on page 96. What details do you notice?
3. Gently close your eyes. Pause.

REFLECT

1. Read Psalm 59:9-13 and then pause. Continue reading Psalm 59:14-17.
2. Notice what words or phrases catch your attention. What emotions are in this passage? Which emotions do you most resonate with?
3. Who are your enemies? How do their actions affect you?
4. How does the author distinguish between himself and his actions and those of his enemies? What role does God play for the author in this passage?
5. Look at the photograph.
6. What can the woman see? What does the mirror do in this image? How does this image help you understand this passage differently? You may see your viewpoint as that of the woman, the mirror, or the photograph as a whole. What happens if you only see from one vantage point? How does that affect the way you think about God?

RESPOND

1. Read Psalm 59:9-13 again. Pause. Continue reading Psalm 59:14-17.
2. Tell God how you see the actions of your enemies, and then confess the ways that you behave in the same manner. Tell God how you would like your enemies to be treated, how you would enact justice, and then ask God to show you a fuller picture of God's love for you and your enemies.
3. Turn your focus away from what your enemies are doing and back to God. Listen to God's invitation to a daily practice of praise and gratitude.
4. Pause.

REST

1. Read Psalm 59:9-13 and then pause. Continue reading Psalm 59:14-17.
2. Inhale. Exhale.
3. Take in God's strength and love with each breath. Exhale anger and judgment.

61

For the choir director: A psalm of David,
to be accompanied by stringed instruments.

1 O God, listen to my cry!
  Hear my prayer!
2 From the ends of the earth,
  I cry to you for help
  when my heart is overwhelmed.
  Lead me to the towering rock of safety,
3 for you are my safe refuge,
  a fortress where my enemies cannot reach me.
4 Let me live forever in your sanctuary,
  safe beneath the shelter of your wings!
  Interlude
5 For you have heard my vows, O God.
  You have given me an inheritance reserved for
  those who fear your name.
6 Add many years to the life of the king!
  May his years span the generations!
7 May he reign under God's protection forever.
  May your unfailing love and faithfulness
  watch over him.
8 Then I will sing praises to your name forever
  as I fulfill my vows each day.

62

For Jeduthun, the choir director:
A psalm of David.

1 I wait quietly before God,
  for my victory comes from him.
2 He alone is my rock and my salvation,
  my fortress where I will never be shaken.
3 So many enemies against one man—
  all of them trying to kill me.
  To them I'm just a broken-down wall
  or a tottering fence.
4 They plan to topple me from my high position.
  They delight in telling lies about me.
  They praise me to my face
  but curse me in their hearts.
  Interlude
5 Let all that I am wait quietly before God,
  for my hope is in him.
6 He alone is my rock and my salvation,
  my fortress where I will not be shaken.
7 My victory and honor come from God alone.
  He is my refuge, a rock where no enemy
  can reach me.
8 O my people, trust in him at all times.
  Pour out your heart to him,
  for God is our refuge.
  Interlude
9 Common people are as worthless
  as a puff of wind, and the powerful are not
  what they appear to be.
  If you weigh them on the scales,
  together they are lighter than a breath of air.
10 Don't make your living by extortion
   or put your hope in stealing.
   And if your wealth increases,
   don't make it the center of your life.
11 God has spoken plainly,
   and I have heard it many times:
   Power, O God, belongs to you;
12 unfailing love, O Lord, is yours.
   Surely you repay all people
   according to what they have done.

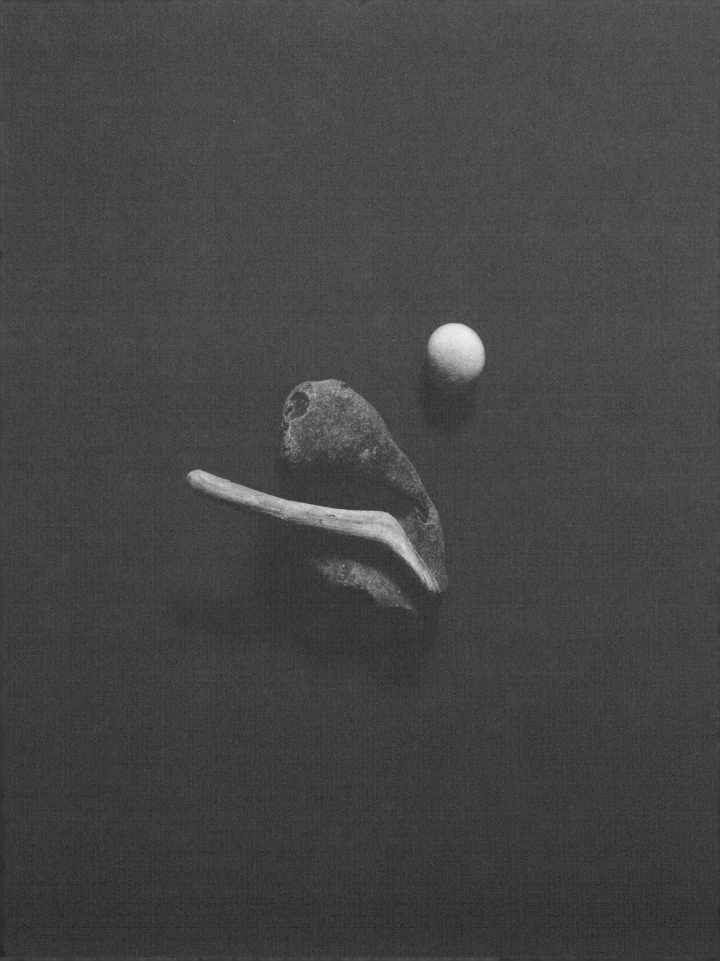

63

A psalm of David, regarding a time when
David was in the wilderness of Judah.

¹ O God, you are my God;
   I earnestly search for you.
   My soul thirsts for you;
      my whole body longs for you
   in this parched and weary land
      where there is no water.

² I have seen you in your sanctuary
      and gazed upon your power and glory.

³ Your unfailing love is better than life itself;
      how I praise you!

⁴ I will praise you as long as I live,
      lifting up my hands to you in prayer.

⁵ You satisfy me more than the richest feast.
   I will praise you with songs of joy.

⁶ I lie awake thinking of you,
      meditating on you through the night.

⁷ Because you are my helper,
   I sing for joy in the shadow of your wings.

⁸ I cling to you;
      your strong right hand holds me securely.

⁹ But those plotting to destroy me will come to ruin.
   They will go down into the depths of the earth.

¹⁰ They will die by the sword
      and become the food of jackals.

¹¹ But the king will rejoice in God.
   All who swear to tell the truth will praise him,
      while liars will be silenced.

LONGING

PSALM 63:1-8

READ

1. Read Psalm 63:1-8 slowly.
2. Pause.
3. Look at the photograph on page 102. Notice the details in this landscape.
4. Pause.

REFLECT

1. Read the passage, aloud if possible. Read it slowly and notice what words and phrases you resonate with. What words and images capture your imagination?
2. Pause.
3. Look at the photograph. Imagine yourself somewhere in this landscape. How do you feel? Is the land parched and scary, powerful and glorious? What do you want to do in this landscape? Where is God in this photograph?
4. Pause.
5. The psalmist refers to God's sanctuary in verse 2. Where in this image do you see or experience sanctuary?
6. How do you know when your body longs for God? How does that feel and what do you do to answer that physical longing for God?

7. The psalmist writes about meditation in verse 6. What practices connecting the body to the spirit and mind is God inviting you to explore? What could a physical practice of praise look like?

RESPOND

1. Read the passage again.
2. Change your physical posture. Stand or kneel if you are able. Praise God, aloud if possible, moving as you sing for joy; cling to God.
3. Think back to the last incredible meal you enjoyed. Describe that rich feast (v. 5), and then think about the ways God satisfies you that even the richest feast cannot.
4. Imagine again being in the photograph. What needs does God meet for us in nature? In a space where there is no water or food? What is God offering us, showing us through creation?

REST

1. Read the passage a final time.
2. Sit in silence knowing wherever you are is God's sanctuary for you.

64

For the choir director: A psalm of David.

¹ O God, listen to my complaint.
  Protect my life from my enemies' threats.
² Hide me from the plots of this evil mob,
  from this gang of wrongdoers.
³ They sharpen their tongues like swords
  and aim their bitter words like arrows.
⁴ They shoot from ambush at the innocent,
  attacking suddenly and fearlessly.
⁵ They encourage each other to do evil
  and plan how to set their traps in secret.
  "Who will ever notice?" they ask.
⁶ As they plot their crimes, they say,
  "We have devised the perfect plan!"
  Yes, the human heart and mind are cunning.
⁷ But God himself will shoot them with his arrows,
  suddenly striking them down.
⁸ Their own tongues will ruin them,
  and all who see them will shake their heads in scorn.
⁹ Then everyone will be afraid;
  they will proclaim the mighty acts of God
  and realize all the amazing things he does.
¹⁰ The godly will rejoice in the LORD
  and find shelter in him.
  And those who do what is right will praise him.

65

For the choir director: A song. A psalm of David.

¹ What mighty praise, O God, belongs to you in Zion.
  We will fulfill our vows to you,

² for you answer our prayers.
  All of us must come to you.
³ Though we are overwhelmed by our sins,
  you forgive them all.
⁴ What joy for those you choose to bring near,
  those who live in your holy courts.
  What festivities await us inside your holy Temple.
⁵ You faithfully answer our prayers
  with awesome deeds,
  O God our savior.
  You are the hope of everyone on earth,
  even those who sail on distant seas.
⁶ You formed the mountains by your power
  and armed yourself with mighty strength.
⁷ You quieted the raging oceans
  with their pounding waves
  and silenced the shouting of the nations.
⁸ Those who live at the ends of the earth
  stand in awe of your wonders.
  From where the sun rises to where it sets,
  you inspire shouts of joy.
⁹ You take care of the earth and water it,
  making it rich and fertile.
  The river of God has plenty of water;
  it provides a bountiful harvest of grain,
  for you have ordered it so.
¹⁰ You drench the plowed ground with rain,
  melting the clods and leveling the ridges.
  You soften the earth with showers
  and bless its abundant crops.
¹¹ You crown the year with a bountiful harvest;
  even the hard pathways overflow with abundance.
¹² The grasslands of the wilderness
  become a lush pasture,
  and the hillsides blossom with joy.
¹³ The meadows are clothed with flocks of sheep,
  and the valleys are carpeted with grain.
  They all shout and sing for joy!

66

For the choir director: A song. A psalm.

1 Shout joyful praises to God, all the earth!
2 Sing about the glory of his name!
   Tell the world how glorious he is.
3 Say to God, "How awesome are your deeds!
   Your enemies cringe before your mighty power.
4 Everything on earth will worship you;
   they will sing your praises,
   shouting your name in glorious songs."
   Interlude
5 Come and see what our God has done,
   what awesome miracles he performs for people!
6 He made a dry path through the Red Sea,
   and his people went across on foot.
   There we rejoiced in him.
7 For by his great power he rules forever.
   He watches every movement of the nations;
   let no rebel rise in defiance.
   Interlude
8 Let the whole world bless our God
   and loudly sing his praises.
9 Our lives are in his hands,
   and he keeps our feet from stumbling.
10 You have tested us, O God;
   you have purified us like silver.

11 You captured us in your net
   and laid the burden of slavery on our backs.
12 Then you put a leader over us.
   We went through fire and flood,
   but you brought us to a place of great abundance.
13 Now I come to your Temple with burnt offerings
   to fulfill the vows I made to you—
14 yes, the sacred vows that I made
   when I was in deep trouble.
15 That is why I am sacrificing
   burnt offerings to you—
   the best of my rams as a pleasing aroma,
   and a sacrifice of bulls and male goats.
   Interlude
16 Come and listen, all you who fear God,
   and I will tell you what he did for me.
17 For I cried out to him for help,
   praising him as I spoke.
18 If I had not confessed the sin in my heart,
   the Lord would not have listened.
19 But God did listen!
   He paid attention to my prayer.
20 Praise God, who did not ignore my prayer
   or withdraw his unfailing love from me.

67

For the choir director: A song. A psalm, to be accompanied by stringed instruments.

1 May God be merciful and bless us.
  May his face smile with favor on us.
2 May your ways be known throughout the earth,
  your saving power among people everywhere.
3 May the nations praise you, O God.
  Yes, may all the nations praise you.
4 Let the whole world sing for joy,
  because you govern the nations with justice
  and guide the people of the whole world.
  Interlude
5 May the nations praise you, O God.
  Yes, may all the nations praise you.
6 Then the earth will yield its harvests,
  and God, our God, will richly bless us.
7 Yes, God will bless us,
  and people all over the world will fear him.

68

For the choir director: A song. A psalm of David.

1 Rise up, O God, and scatter your enemies.
  Let those who hate God run for their lives.
2 Blow them away like smoke.
  Melt them like wax in a fire.
  Let the wicked perish in the presence of God.
3 But let the godly rejoice.
  Let them be glad in God's presence.
  Let them be filled with joy.
4 Sing praises to God and to his name!
  Sing loud praises to him who rides the clouds.
  His name is the LORD—rejoice in his presence!
5 Father to the fatherless, defender of widows—
  this is God, whose dwelling is holy.
6 God places the lonely in families;
  he sets the prisoners free and gives them joy.
  But he makes the rebellious
  live in a sun-scorched land.

7 O God, when you led your people out from Egypt,
  when you marched through the dry wasteland,
  Interlude

8 the earth trembled, and the heavens
  poured down rain
  before you, the God of Sinai,
  before God, the God of Israel.

9 You sent abundant rain, O God,
  to refresh the weary land.

10 There your people finally settled,
   and with a bountiful harvest, O God,
   you provided for your needy people.

11 The Lord gives the word,
   and a great army brings the good news.

12 Enemy kings and their armies flee,
   while the women of Israel divide the plunder.

13 Even those who lived among
   the sheepfolds found treasures—
   doves with wings of silver and feathers of gold.

14 The Almighty scattered the enemy kings
   like a blowing snowstorm on Mount Zalmon.

15 The mountains of Bashan are majestic,
   with many peaks stretching high into the sky.

16 Why do you look with envy, O rugged mountains,
   at Mount Zion, where God has chosen to live,
   where the LORD himself will live forever?

17 Surrounded by unnumbered thousands of chariots,
   the Lord came from Mount Sinai into his sanctuary.

18 When you ascended to the heights,
   you led a crowd of captives.
   You received gifts from the people,
   even from those who rebelled against you.
   Now the LORD God will live among us there.

19 Praise the Lord; praise God our savior!
   For each day he carries us in his arms.
   Interlude

20 Our God is a God who saves!
   The Sovereign LORD rescues us from death.

21 But God will smash the heads of his enemies,
   crushing the skulls of those who love their guilty ways.

22 The Lord says, "I will bring
   my enemies down from Bashan;
   I will bring them up from the depths of the sea.

23 You, my people, will wash your feet in their blood,
   and even your dogs will get their share!"

24 Your procession has come into view, O God—
   the procession of my God and King
   as he goes into the sanctuary.

25 Singers are in front, musicians behind;
   between them are young women
   playing tambourines.

26 Praise God, all you people of Israel;
   praise the LORD, the source of Israel's life.

27 Look, the little tribe of Benjamin leads the way.
   Then comes a great throng of rulers from Judah
   and all the rulers of Zebulun and Naphtali.

28 Summon your might, O God.
   Display your power, O God, as you have in the past.

29 The kings of the earth are bringing tribute
   to your Temple in Jerusalem.

30 Rebuke these enemy nations—
   these wild animals lurking in the reeds,
   this herd of bulls among the weaker calves.
   Make them bring bars of silver in humble tribute.
   Scatter the nations that delight in war.

31 Let Egypt come with gifts of precious metals;
   let Ethiopia bring tribute to God.

32 Sing to God, you kingdoms of the earth.
   Sing praises to the Lord.
   Interlude

33 Sing to the one who rides across
   the ancient heavens,
   his mighty voice thundering from the sky.

34 Tell everyone about God's power.
   His majesty shines down on Israel;
   his strength is mighty in the heavens.

35 God is awesome in his sanctuary.
   The God of Israel gives power
   and strength to his people.
   Praise be to God!

69

For the choir director: A psalm of David,
to be sung to the tune "Lilies."

1 Save me, O God,
for the floodwaters are up to my neck.
2 Deeper and deeper I sink into the mire;
I can't find a foothold.
I am in deep water,
and the floods overwhelm me.
3 I am exhausted from crying for help;
my throat is parched.
My eyes are swollen with weeping,
waiting for my God to help me.
4 Those who hate me without cause
outnumber the hairs on my head.
Many enemies try to destroy me with lies,
demanding that I give back what I didn't steal.
5 O God, you know how foolish I am;
my sins cannot be hidden from you.
6 Don't let those who trust in you
be ashamed because of me,
O Sovereign LORD of Heaven's Armies.
Don't let me cause them to be humiliated,

O God of Israel.
7 For I endure insults for your sake;
humiliation is written all over my face.
8 Even my own brothers
pretend they don't know me;
they treat me like a stranger.
9 Passion for your house has consumed me,
and the insults of those
who insult you have fallen on me.
10 When I weep and fast,
they scoff at me.
11 When I dress in burlap to show sorrow,
they make fun of me.
12 I am the favorite topic of town gossip,
and all the drunks sing about me.
13 But I keep praying to you, LORD,
hoping this time you will show me favor.
In your unfailing love, O God,
answer my prayer with your sure salvation.
14 Rescue me from the mud;

don't let me sink any deeper!
Save me from those who hate me,
and pull me from these deep waters.
15 Don't let the floods overwhelm me,
or the deep waters swallow me,
or the pit of death devour me.
16 Answer my prayers, O LORD,
for your unfailing love is wonderful.
Take care of me,
for your mercy is so plentiful.
17 Don't hide from your servant;
answer me quickly, for I am in deep trouble!
18 Come and redeem me;
free me from my enemies.
19 You know of my shame, scorn, and disgrace.
You see all that my enemies are doing.
20 Their insults have broken my heart,
and I am in despair.
If only one person would show some pity;
if only one would turn and comfort me.
21 But instead, they give me poison for food;
they offer me sour wine for my thirst.
22 Let the bountiful table set before them
become a snare
and their prosperity become a trap.
23 Let their eyes go blind so they cannot see,
and make their bodies shake continually.
24 Pour out your fury on them;
consume them with your burning anger.
25 Let their homes become desolate

and their tents be deserted.
26 To the one you have punished,
they add insult to injury;
they add to the pain of those you have hurt.
27 Pile their sins up high,
and don't let them go free.
28 Erase their names from the Book of Life;
don't let them be counted among the righteous.
29 I am suffering and in pain.
Rescue me, O God, by your saving power.
30 Then I will praise God's name with singing,
and I will honor him with thanksgiving.
31 For this will please the LORD
more than sacrificing cattle,
more than presenting a bull
with its horns and hooves.
32 The humble will see their God
at work and be glad.
Let all who seek God's help be encouraged.
33 For the Lord hears the cries of the needy;
he does not despise his imprisoned people.
34 Praise him, O heaven and earth,
the seas and all that move in them.
35 For God will save Jerusalem
and rebuild the towns of Judah.
His people will live there
and settle in their own land.
36 The descendants of those who obey him
will inherit the land,
and those who love him will live there in safety.

OVERWHELM ME

PSALM 69:1-6

READ

1. Read Psalm 69:1-6.
2. Pause.
3. Look at the photograph on pages 110-11. What do you notice?

REFLECT

1. Read the passage, aloud if possible. Notice what stands out to you. What words or phrases do you resonate with? Notice if your emotions shift as you read the passage.
2. Pause.
3. Look again at the photograph that serves as the background to this passage. Notice the photograph is blurry, capturing motion but leaving the overall image unclear. Notice the lighting and what that allows you to see but also that it obscures your view of the space.
4. Pause.
5. Read the passage slowly.

6. If you find yourself resonating with one of the verses, sit with the thoughts and emotions that are coming to the surface.
7. What is God's invitation to you in this moment?

RESPOND

1. Tell God how you are feeling. Are you exhausted? Drowning? Ashamed? Accept God's invitation to name your emotions, feel your feelings, and so on.

REST

1. Read the passage once again.
2. Gently close your eyes. Inhale God's promises. Exhale the weight of any emotions you are experiencing.
3. Allow yourself time to rest, taking a nap if you are able and notice your body needs it. Remember, God is not afraid of your emotions.

70

For the choir director: A psalm of David,
asking God to remember him.

1 Please, God, rescue me!
Come quickly, LORD, and help me.
2 May those who try to kill me
be humiliated and put to shame.
May those who take delight in my trouble
be turned back in disgrace.
3 Let them be horrified by their shame,
for they said, "Aha! We've got him now!"
4 But may all who search for you
be filled with joy and gladness in you.
May those who love your salvation
repeatedly shout, "God is great!"
5 But as for me, I am poor and needy;
please hurry to my aid, O God.
You are my helper and my savior;
O LORD, do not delay.

71

¹ O Lord, I have come to you for protection;
don't let me be disgraced.

² Save me and rescue me,
for you do what is right.
Turn your ear to listen to me,
and set me free.

³ Be my rock of safety
where I can always hide.
Give the order to save me,
for you are my rock and my fortress.

⁴ My God, rescue me from
the power of the wicked,
from the clutches of cruel oppressors.

⁵ O Lord, you alone are my hope.
I've trusted you, O Lord, from childhood.

⁶ Yes, you have been with me from birth;
from my mother's womb you have cared for me.
No wonder I am always praising you!

⁷ My life is an example to many,
because you have been
my strength and protection.

⁸ That is why I can never stop praising you;
I declare your glory all day long.

⁹ And now, in my old age, don't set me aside.
Don't abandon me when my strength is failing.

¹⁰ For my enemies are whispering against me.
They are plotting together to kill me.

¹¹ They say, "God has abandoned him.
Let's go and get him,
for no one will help him now."

¹² O God, don't stay away.
My God, please hurry to help me.

¹³ Bring disgrace and destruction on my accusers.
Humiliate and shame those who want to harm me.

¹⁴ But I will keep on hoping for your help;
I will praise you more and more.

¹⁵ I will tell everyone about your righteousness.
All day long I will proclaim your saving power,
though I am not skilled with words.

¹⁶ I will praise your mighty deeds,
O Sovereign Lord.
I will tell everyone that you alone are just.

¹⁷ O God, you have taught me
from my earliest childhood,
and I constantly tell others
about the wonderful things you do.

¹⁸ Now that I am old and gray,
do not abandon me, O God.
Let me proclaim your power
to this new generation,
your mighty miracles to all who come after me.

¹⁹ Your righteousness, O God,
reaches to the highest heavens.
You have done such wonderful things.
Who can compare with you, O God?

²⁰ You have allowed me to suffer much hardship,
but you will restore me to life again
and lift me up from the depths of the earth.

²¹ You will restore me to even greater honor
and comfort me once again.

²² Then I will praise you with music on the harp,
because you are faithful to your promises,
O my God.
I will sing praises to you with a lyre,
O Holy One of Israel.

²³ I will shout for joy and sing your praises,

for you have ransomed me.
²⁴ I will tell about your righteous deeds
all day long,
for everyone who tried to hurt me
has been shamed and humiliated.

72

A psalm of Solomon.

¹ Give your love of justice to the king, O God,
and righteousness to the king's son.
² Help him judge your people in the right way;
let the poor always be treated fairly.
³ May the mountains yield prosperity for all,
and may the hills be fruitful.
⁴ Help him to defend the poor,
to rescue the children of the needy,
and to crush their oppressors.
⁵ May they fear you as long as the sun shines,
as long as the moon remains in the sky.
Yes, forever!
⁶ May the king's rule be refreshing
like spring rain on freshly cut grass,
like the showers that water the earth.
⁷ May all the godly flourish during his reign.
May there be abundant prosperity
until the moon is no more.
⁸ May he reign from sea to sea,
and from the Euphrates River
to the ends of the earth.
⁹ Desert nomads will bow before him;
his enemies will fall before him in the dust.

¹⁰ The western kings of Tarshish
and other distant lands
will bring him tribute.
The eastern kings of Sheba and Seba
will bring him gifts.
¹¹ All kings will bow before him,
and all nations will serve him.
¹² He will rescue the poor when they cry to him;
he will help the oppressed,
who have no one to defend them.
¹³ He feels pity for the weak and the needy,
and he will rescue them.
¹⁴ He will redeem them
from oppression and violence,
for their lives are precious to him.
¹⁵ Long live the king!
May the gold of Sheba be given to him.
May the people always pray for him
and bless him all day long.
¹⁶ May there be abundant grain
throughout the land,
flourishing even on the hilltops.
May the fruit trees flourish
like the trees of Lebanon,
and may the people thrive like grass in a field.
¹⁷ May the king's name endure forever;
may it continue as long as the sun shines.
May all nations be blessed through him
and bring him praise.
¹⁸ Praise the LORD God, the God of Israel,
who alone does such wonderful things.
¹⁹ Praise his glorious name forever!
Let the whole earth be filled with his glory.
Amen and amen!
²⁰ (This ends the prayers of David son of Jesse.)

IMAGINE FLOURISHING

PSALM 72:1-7

READ

1. Read Psalm 72:1-7.
2. Pause.

REFLECT

1. Read the passage slowly, and aloud if possible.
2. Notice if you resonate with specific words or phrases. What stands out to you?
3. This psalm is as much a song as it is a prayer intercession. Do you find yourself in this passage, relating to one request of God more than the others? What call to justice or desire for blessing do you most desire?
4. What is justice to you? What does prosperity for all look like? What would flourishing look like for you? Your family? Your community?
5. What, if anything, do you sense God is inviting you to do? To feel? To invite others into?

RESPOND

1. Talk with God about the injustices and inequities you see and how you would like God to address them. Tell God about your dreams for justice and flourishing, and how that would look in everyday life.
2. Ask God to help you understand what you are being invited into to bring about that justice and flourishing.

REST

1. Read the passage again.
2. Pause.
3. Sit with the image of a world of flourishing for everyone. Take in the feeling of that joy and justice. If you wish, hold out your hands as if accepting the invitation to participate in God's work of abundance and prosperity.

LIST OF GUIDED MEDITATIONS

CONTINUE THE CONVERSATION

www.alabasterco.com